Speaking First

Ten practice tests for the **Cambridge B2 First**

Luis Porras Wadley

www.prosperityeducation.net

PROSPERITY EDUCATION
www.prosperityeducation.net

Registered offices: Sherlock Close, Cambridge
CB3 0HP, United Kingdom

© Prosperity Education Ltd. 2019

First published 2019

ISBN: 978-1-9161297-0-2

Manufactured on demand by KDP.

All rights reserved. No part of this book may be reprinted or reproduced or utilised in any form or by any electronic, mechanical, or other means, now known or hereafter invented, including photocopying and recording, or in any information storage or retrieval system, without permission in writing from Prosperity Education.

The right of Luis Porras Wadley to be identified as the author has been asserted in accordance with sections 77 and 78 of the Copyright, Designs and Patents Act 1988.

'Cambridge B2 First' and 'FCE' are brands belonging to The Chancellor, Masters and Scholars of the University of Cambridge and are not associated with Prosperity Education or its products.

For further information and resources, visit:
www.prosperityeducation.net

To infinity and beyond.

Contents

Introduction		4
Frequently asked questions		6
Speaking Test 1		**9**
1:	Holidays and travelling; Free time; Television	10
2:	1 Spending time together; 2 Eating out	11
3 & 4:	Choosing a place to study	14
Speaking Test 2		**17**
1:	Studying; Celebrations; The internet and social media	18
2:	1 Explanations; 2 Jobs	19
3 & 4:	Taking up a sport	22
Speaking Test 3		**25**
1:	Music; Eating out; Friends	26
2:	1 Couples on holiday; 2 College life	27
3 & 4:	Choosing an artistic career	30
Speaking Test 4		**33**
1:	Shopping; Cooking; Employment	34
2:	1 Reading carefully; 2 Spending time outdoors	35
3 & 4:	Using the internet	38
Speaking Test 5		**41**
1:	Where you live; Emails and letters; College / school	42
2:	1 Working with animals; 2 Receiving presents	43
3 & 4:	Living abroad	46
Speaking Test 6		**49**
1:	Animals and pets; Healthy habits; Keeping in touch	50
2:	1 Waiting patiently; 2 Professionals discussing	51
3 & 4:	Taking care of the environment	54
Speaking Test 7		**57**
1:	Journeys; Arts; Computers	58
2:	1 Trying to concentrate; 2 Doing the shopping	59
3 & 4:	Improving life in the city	62
Speaking Test 8		**65**
1:	Flying; Travelling abroad; Advice	66
2:	1 Learning in different ways; 2 Means of transport	67
3 & 4:	Improving a local college	70
Speaking Test 9		**73**
1:	Celebrities; Extreme sports; Money and jobs	74
2:	1 Taking a break; 2 Using electronic devices	75
3 & 4:	Reducing traffic in cities	78
Speaking Test 10		**81**
1:	Adventure activities; Being at home; Languages	82
2:	1 Spending the weekend; 2 Taking pictures	83
3 & 4:	Young people earning money	86
Model answers to Speaking Test 1		**89**

Introduction

The B2 First exam, formerly known as the First Certificate in English (FCE), is an examination developed by Cambridge Assessment English, which is part of the University of Cambridge.

The B2 First is usually taken by candidates who want to obtain a B2-level certificate, which corresponds to an upper-intermediate level of English. As described by the Common European Framework of Reference for Languages (CEFRL), candidates with a B2 level are considered *independent vantage users*, thus being able to understand the main ideas of complex tests, to interact with a certain degree of fluency and spontaneity, both in written and oral form, and to produce clear and detailed texts on a range of subjects.

This book aims to provide meaningful speaking practice while following the format of the B2 First Speaking paper. Both teachers and candidates can benefit from this resource, in that they can familiarise themselves with the format and level of the exam, and the type of questions and topics covered. Furthermore, and most importantly, students can learn, through repetitive practice, what to expect on the day of their speaking exam.

B2 First: Speaking Parts

The Speaking paper is one of the five papers that comprise the B2 First examination. This section of the exam is taken in pairs, or trios, of candidates, who are assessed by two examiners: the interlocutor and the assessor. The interlocutor is responsible for delivering the instructions, handling the test booklet and interacting with the candidates, while the assessor simply listens and marks each candidate's performance.

The Speaking paper is divided into four parts, all of which comprise a different task. Different degrees of participation are expected from the candidates in each of these tasks.

Part 1

In Part 1, candidates are asked questions mainly about themselves, their background and their experiences. It starts with a set of brief introductory questions (e.g. *...and your names are? Where are you from?*) and continues with one or more topic-based questions. These topics may include things like holidays and travel, leisure-time activities, friends and family, television, etc. To these questions, candidates are expected to provide brief but complete answers.

Timing	2 minutes (pair) / 3 minutes (trio)
Focus	Giving personal information, expressing opinions about various topics and talking about past experiences.
Interaction	Interlocutor – Candidate

Part 2

In Part 2, each candidate is asked to talk about two photographs and also to answer a question about their partner's photographs. Each candidate must compare a pair of pictures and answer a question about those pictures in one minute. Following this, the other candidate is asked a different question related to the pictures themselves or the topic of the pictures (thirty seconds). The pair of photographs and questions is different for each candidate.

Timing	4 minutes (pair) / 6 minutes (trio)
Focus	Describing, comparing, expressing opinions and speculating.
Interaction	Interlocutor – Candidate

Part 3

Part 3 is the main collaborative task of the exam. In this part, candidates are presented with a topic in the form of a question (e.g. *What are the advantages and disadvantages of studying in these places?*) and a few prompts linked to it (e.g. *a bedroom, a friend's house, the library,* etc.). The candidates are then expected to develop a two-minute discussion around the topic, making use, if necessary, of the prompts provided. When the two minutes are up, they are asked to make a decision with regard to the topic (e.g. *…decide what the best place to study is during the final exams period.*). The candidates have one more minute to complete the task.

Timing	4 minutes (pair) / 5 minutes (trio)
Focus	Discussing, exchanging ideas, agreeing and disagreeing, asking for opinions, explaining views, justifying opinions, reaching agreements, making decisions, etc.
Interaction	Interlocutor – Candidate – Candidate

Part 4

In Part 4, candidates are asked some questions which stem from the discussion topic in Part 3. These are questions that normally touch on complex issues like education, learning, healthy habits, careers, new technologies, etc. The candidates are expected to develop extended answers and may be prompted to exchange views rather than answer individually.

Timing	4 minutes (pair) / 6 minutes (trio)
Focus	Exchanging ideas, extending and explaining answers, agreeing and disagreeing and justifying opinions.
Interaction	Interlocutor – Candidate – Candidate

I hope that you will find this resource a useful study aid, and I wish you all the best in preparing for the exam.

Luis Porras Wadley – Granada, 2019

Frequently asked questions

Is the Speaking exam taken individually or in pairs?
The Speaking test is taken in pairs or trios, unless a candidate has special needs that may affect their performance. This may lead to them taking the test individually. However, regular tests are normally taken in pairs, and if there is an uneven number of candidates, only the last three candidates will take the exam as a trio.

Can candidates choose to do the test with a friend or classmate?
This depends on the examination centre candidates register with. Each centre has its own policy and this may or may not be allowed. In the end, it is up to the supervisor of the exam to allow it or not, and the decision will be based on exam timing and logistics rather than candidates' preferences.

Do candidates have to speak with each other at some point?
Yes, they do. Candidates must always speak to each other in Part 3 and usually in Part 4. The rest of the test is carried out individually yet, in their answers, candidates can refer to what the other candidate has said earlier in the test.

How many people are there in the Speaking room?
In the Speaking room there can be up to five people: two examiners and two or three candidates. Occasionally, there may be a third examiner, but their role will not be to assess the candidates.

What happens if the interlocutor interrupts a candidate when the time of a task is over?
This is completely normal and candidates should expect to be interrupted when the time is up. The interlocutor's job involves ensuring that every candidate has the same opportunities to speak, which includes having the same time allocated to do so. If a candidate has developed their answer well and has responded fully, but with time to spare, they will not lose marks.

In Part 3, must candidates reach an agreement by the end of the task?
Not at all. The purpose of the test is to assess candidates' speaking skills, not the completion of the task or the conveyance of their opinions. Candidates are only expected to develop a discussion in which they work towards an agreement or decision by means of exchanging views and opinions, and agreeing and disagreeing. Whether or not they have reached an agreement by the end of the task is irrelevant to their mark.

In Part 3, do candidates have to talk about all the different prompts?
No, this is not necessary. The prompts in this part of the test are there to ensure that candidates have some ideas to talk about and that they engage in a discussion. However, they are not necessarily expected to use all of them, nor are they limited to those prompts; they can bring their own ideas into the discussion.

What do candidates need to take to the Speaking exam?
Candidates need to take a valid form of photographic ID (Passport, National Identity Card, Driver's Licence, etc.) and their Confirmation of Entry, which is a document provided by the examination centre some time before the test.

What are the mark sheets mentioned at the beginning of the exams?
The mark sheets contain each candidate's name, surname and their candidate number, and this is where the assessor writes their marks. These sheets are given to candidates before they enter the examination room, and they will have to give them to the interlocutor at the beginning of the test. The examiners will then keep the mark sheets to relay or send the candidates' marks to Cambridge Assessment English.

Where does the Speaking exam take place?
The Speaking exam can take place in a range of venues, but it is most likely to take place in the examination centre itself (usually a language school) or one of its examination venues, which also tend to be language schools. Some other examination venues may be hotels or conference rooms.

Is the Speaking exam done the same day as the other parts of the test?
Not normally, but it can happen. Given the length of the whole exam, it is usually more practical and reasonable to do the Speaking test on a different day. This is decided by the examination centres and candidates are informed of this well in advance.

Will the examiners be looking at the candidates throughout the whole test?
No, they will not. Examiners, especially the assessor, have to assign marks while the exam is taking place. For this reason, there will be times throughout the test when they might be looking at their examiner booklets or candidate mark sheets instead of the candidates. However, this does not mean that they are not paying attention to the candidates and their responses.

How is the Speaking exam marked?
Each candidate's performance throughout the test is marked both by the interlocutor and the assessor, who give candidates a score for five different categories: grammar and vocabulary, discourse management, pronunciation, interactive communication and global performance. The assessor is responsible for assessing the first four categories, which account for two thirds of the score, and the interlocutor awards the global mark, which comprises one third of the final speaking score.

Can the other candidate's performance affect a candidate's score?
No, it cannot. Although the exam is taken in pairs or trios, candidates are assessed individually and examiners are duly trained to do so, ensuring that both candidates have the same opportunities to speak and thus can be marked separately.

Can I memorise some answers for the exam?
While the introductory questions are common to all tests, candidates are advised not to prepare long answers in advance or to memorise short speeches. Examiners can easily tell when a candidate is using a pre-learned speech and will interrupt them when they feel it is necessary to do so.

Cambridge B2 First Speaking

Test 1

Test 1 – Part 1	Cambridge B2 First: Speaking
2 minutes (3 minutes for groups of three)	

Candidates' background

Good morning/afternoon/evening. My name is …………… and this is my colleague …………… .

And your names are?

Can I have your mark sheets, please?

Thank you.

- Where are you from, *(Candidate A)*?
- And you, *(Candidate B)*?

First, we'd like to know something about you.

Select one or more questions from any of the following categories, as appropriate.

Holidays and travelling

- **When was the last time that you went on holiday? …… (What did you do?)**
- **When you're on holiday, how do you like to travel? …… (Why?)**
- **How often do you travel abroad? …… (Would you like to travel more?) …… (Why?)**
- **Is there a country that you would really like to visit in the future? …… (Why? / Why not?)**

Free time

- **How do you like to spend your free time? …… (Why?)**
- **How much free time do you have? …… (Do you think it's enough?)**
- **Do you prefer to spend your free time alone or with friends? …… (Why?)**
- **Is there a new leisure-time activity you'd like to try? …… (Which one?) …… (Why?)**

Television

- **Do you enjoy watching TV? …… (Why? / Why not?)**
- **Do you think people spend too much time watching TV nowadays? …… (Why? / Why not?)**
- **Have you ever appeared on TV? (Tell us about it.)**
- **Is there a programme you particularly enjoy watching? …… (Tell us about it.)**

Cambridge B2 First: Speaking

Test 1 – Part 2
4 minutes (6 minutes for groups of three)

1 Spending time together	2 Eating out

Interlocutor — In this part of the test, I'm going to give each of you two photographs. I'd like you to talk about your photographs on your own for about a minute, and also to answer a question about your partner's photographs.

(Candidate A), it's your turn first. Here are your photographs. They show **people spending time together**.

Place Part 2 Task 1, in front of Candidate A.

I'd like you to compare the photographs, and say **what you think the people are enjoying about spending time together**.

All right?

Candidate A

1 minute

Interlocutor — Thank you.

(Candidate B), **do you often spend time with your family? …… (Why? / Why not?)**

Candidate B

Approximately 30 seconds

Interlocutor — Thank you. (Can I have the booklet, please?) *Retrieve Part 2 Task 1.*

Now, *(Candidate B)*, here are your photographs. They show **people having lunch in different places**.

Place Part 2 Task 2, in front of Candidate B.

I'd like you to compare the photographs, and say **why you think the people have chosen to eat in these places**.

All right?

Candidate B

1 minute

Interlocutor — Thank you.

(Candidate A), **where do you usually eat with your friends? …… (Why?)**

Candidate A

Approximately 30 seconds

Interlocutor — Thank you. (Can I have the booklet, please?) *Retrieve Part 2 Task 2.*

Cambridge B2 First and FCE are brands belonging to The University of Cambridge and are not associated with Prosperity Education

Test 1 – Part 2
Task 1

Cambridge B2 First: Speaking

What are the people enjoying about spending time together?

Cambridge B2 First: Speaking

Test 1 – Part 2
Task 2

Why have the people chosen to eat in these places?

Test 1 – Part 3
4 minutes (5 minutes for groups of three)

Cambridge B2 First: Speaking

Choosing a place to study

Interlocutor Now, I'd like you to talk about something together for about two minutes *(3 minutes for groups of three)*.

Here are some places where people sometimes choose to study and a question for you to discuss. First you have some time to look at the task.

*Place **Part 3 Task 3**, in front of the candidates. Allow 15 seconds.*

Now, talk to each other about **the advantages and disadvantages of studying in these places**.

Candidate A

....

2 minutes (3 minutes for groups of three)

Interlocutor Thank you. Now you have about a minute to decide **what is the best place to study during the exam periods**.

Candidate B

....

Approximately 30 seconds

Interlocutor Thank you. (Can I have the booklet, please?) *Retrieve **Part 3 Task 3**.*

Part 4
4 minutes (6 minutes for groups of three)

Interlocutor *Use the following questions, in order, as appropriate:*

- Do you think that we study the right subjects at school? …… (Why? / Why not?)

- Some people say it's more important to study science than history. What's your opinion?

- Some people believe that practical experience is more useful than studying theory. Do you agree? …… (Why? / Why not?)

- Do you believe teachers should be paid a higher salary than sportspeople? …… (Why? / Why not?)

- Some people say that teachers and children get too many holidays. What do you think?

- Do you think that parents and teachers have the same responsibility in children's education? …… (Why? / Why not?)

Select any of the following prompts, as appropriate:
- What do you think?
- Do you agree?
- And you?

Interlocutor Thank you. That is the end of the test.

Cambridge B2 First: Speaking

Test 1 – Part 3
Task 3

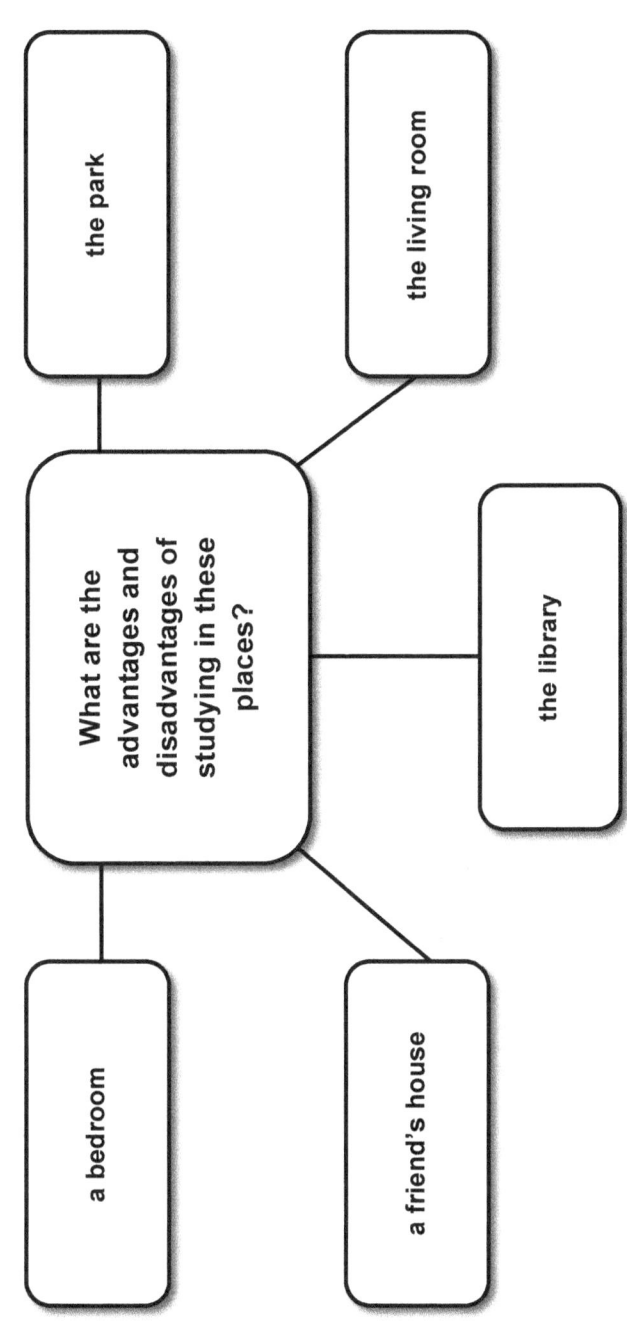

Mark sheet			Cambridge B2 First: Speaking

DD	MM	YY

Candidate	

Marks awarded

Grammar and vocabulary	0	1	1.5	2	2.5	3	3.5	4	4.5	5
Discourse management	0	1	1.5	2	2.5	3	3.5	4	4.5	5
Pronunciation	0	1	1.5	2	2.5	3	3.5	4	4.5	5
Interactive communication	0	1	1.5	2	2.5	3	3.5	4	4.5	5

Item descriptors

Grammar and vocabulary	• Degree of control of grammatical forms.
	• Range of vocabulary used to give and exchange views.
Discourse management	• Stretches of language produced.
	• Relevance of contributions and organisation of ideas.
	• Use of appropriate cohesive devices and discourse markers.
Pronunciation	• Intelligibility
	• Intonation
	• Word stress
	• Individual sounds
Interactive communication	• Initiating, responding and linking contributions to those of other speakers.
	• Maintaining and developing interaction, and negotiating.

Assessment notes

Cambridge B2 First Speaking

Test 2

Test 2 – Part 1	Cambridge B2 First: Speaking
2 minutes (3 minutes for groups of three)	

Candidates' background

Good morning/afternoon/evening. My name is …………… and this is my colleague …………… .

And your names are?

Can I have your mark sheets, please?

Thank you.

- Where are you from, *(Candidate A)*?
- And you, *(Candidate B)*?

First, we'd like to know something about you.

Select one or more questions from any of the following categories, as appropriate.

Studying

- **How often do you have to study nowadays? …… (Why? / Why not?)**
- **If you had the chance, what would you like to study in the future? …… (Why? / Why not?)**
- **Do you think it's useful to study a foreign language? …… (Why / Why not?)**
- **In your opinion, what's the worst thing about studying? …… (Why?)**

Celebrations

- **Do you enjoy family celebrations? …… (Why? / Why not?)**
- **How did you celebrate your last birthday? …… (Did you enjoy yourself?)**
- **How do you celebrate New Year's Eve? …… (Do you like it?) …… (Why? / Why not?)**
- **Are there any traditional celebrations in your country? …… (What are they?)**

The internet and social media

- **Do you use the internet much? …… (Why? / Why not?)**
- **Tell us about a website you visit regularly. …… (Why do you visit it?)**
- **Do you and your friends communicate online? …… (How do you communicate?)**
- **What's your favourite social networking site? …… (Why?)**

Cambridge B2 First: Speaking	Test 2 – Part 2
	4 minutes (6 minutes for groups of three)

1 Explanations	2 Jobs

Interlocutor In this part of the test, I'm going to give each of you two photographs. I'd like you to talk about your photographs on your own for about a minute, and also to answer a question about your partner's photographs.

(Candidate A), it's your turn first. Here are your photographs. They show **people explaining something to others**.

Place Part 2 Task 1, in front of Candidate A.

I'd like you to compare the photographs, and say **what you think the people might be explaining**.

All right?

Candidate A

1 minute

Interlocutor Thank you.

(Candidate B), **which explanation do you think is the most important? ...... (Why?)**

Candidate B

Approximately 30 seconds

Interlocutor Thank you. (Can I have the booklet, please?) *Retrieve Part 2 Task 1.*

Now, *(Candidate B)*, here are your photographs. They show **people doing different jobs**.

Place Part 2 Task 2, in front of Candidate B.

I'd like you to compare the photographs, and say **what you think the people are enjoying about their job**.

All right?

Candidate B

1 minute

Interlocutor Thank you.

(Candidate A), **which job would you prefer to do? ...... (Why? / Why not?)**

Candidate A

Approximately 30 seconds

Interlocutor Thank you. (Can I have the booklet, please?) *Retrieve Part 2 Task 2.*

Test 2 – Part 2
Task 1

Cambridge B2 First: Speaking

What might the people be explaining?

Cambridge B2 First: Speaking

Test 2 – Part 2
Task 2

What are the people enjoying about their job?

Test 2 – Part 3
4 minutes (5 minutes for groups of three)

Cambridge B2 First: Speaking

Taking up a sport

Interlocutor	Now, I'd like you to talk about something together for about two minutes *(3 minutes for groups of three)*.
	Here are some reasons why people decide to take up a sport and a question for you to discuss. First you have some time to look at the task.
	*Place **Part 3 Task 3**, in front of the candidates. Allow 15 seconds.*
	Now, talk to each other about **why most people decide to take up a sport**.
Candidate A	

2 minutes (3 minutes for groups of three)

Interlocutor	Thank you. Now you have about a minute to decide **what is the best reason for people to take up a new sport**.
Candidate B	

Approximately 30 seconds

Interlocutor	Thank you. (Can I have the booklet, please?) *Retrieve **Part 3 Task 3**.*

Part 4
4 minutes (6 minutes for groups of three)

Interlocutor   *Use the following questions, in order, as appropriate:*

- What are the advantages and disadvantages of doing exercise on a regular basis?

- In your opinion, is it better to do many sports or just one? ...... (Why?)

- Some people think that gyms are the best place to do exercise and get fit. What do you think? ...... (Why? / Why not?)

- Why do you think some people enjoy doing dangerous sports?

- Some people believe that sportspeople are good role models for children. Do you agree? ...... (Why? / Why not?)

- Do you think that doing Physical Education at school is important? ...... (Why? / Why not?)

Select any of the following prompts, as appropriate:

- What do you think?
- Do you agree?
- And you?

Interlocutor   Thank you. That is the end of the test.

Cambridge B2 First: Speaking

Test 2 – Part 3
Task 3

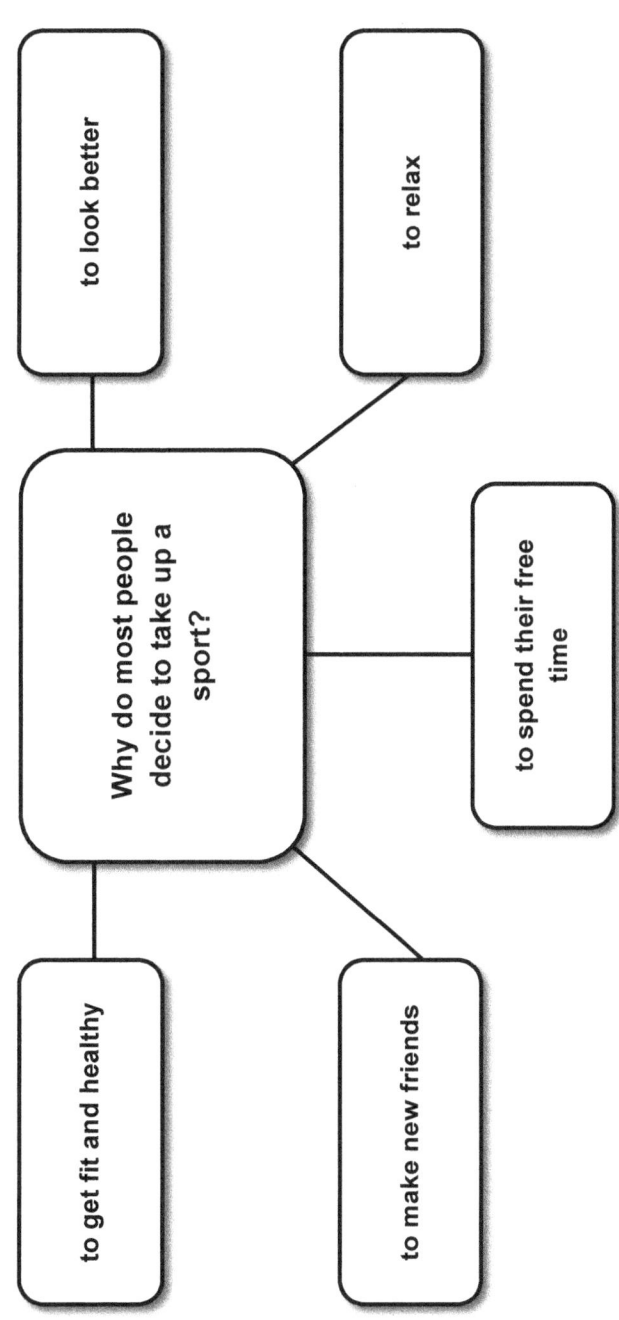

| Mark sheet | Cambridge B2 First: Speaking |

DD	MM	YY

Candidate	

Marks awarded

Grammar and vocabulary	0	1	1.5	2	2.5	3	3.5	4	4.5	5
Discourse management	0	1	1.5	2	2.5	3	3.5	4	4.5	5
Pronunciation	0	1	1.5	2	2.5	3	3.5	4	4.5	5
Interactive communication	0	1	1.5	2	2.5	3	3.5	4	4.5	5

Item descriptors

Grammar and vocabulary	• Degree of control of grammatical forms.
	• Range of vocabulary used to give and exchange views.
Discourse management	• Stretches of language produced.
	• Relevance of contributions and organisation of ideas.
	• Use of appropriate cohesive devices and discourse markers.
Pronunciation	• Intelligibility
	• Intonation
	• Word stress
	• Individual sounds
Interactive communication	• Initiating, responding and linking contributions to those of other speakers.
	• Maintaining and developing interaction, and negotiating.

Assessment notes

Cambridge B2 First Speaking

Test 3

Test 3 – Part 1	Cambridge B2 First: Speaking
2 minutes (3 minutes for groups of three)	

Candidates' background

Good morning/afternoon/evening. My name is …………… and this is my colleague …………… .

And your names are?

Can I have your mark sheets, please?

Thank you.

- Where are you from, *(Candidate A)*?
- And you, *(Candidate B)*?

First, we'd like to know something about you.

Select one or more questions from any of the following categories, as appropriate.

Music

- **Do you listen to music every day? …… (Why? / Why not?)**
- **Is music important in your life? …… (Why? / Why not?)**
- **Do you ever go to live concerts? …… (Why? / Why not?)**
- **What types of music do you listen to when you need to relax?**

Eating out

- **How often do you eat in a restaurant? …… (Would you like to eat out more often?)**
- **Do you prefer to eat out or at home? …… (Why?)**
- **Who do you normally eat out with? …… (Why?)**
- **Do you enjoy cooking for yourself at home? …… (Why? / Why not?)**

Friends

- **Do you still have the same friends you had when you were younger? …… (Why? / Why not?)**
- **Do most of your friends live near you? …… (Why? / Why not?)**
- **How often do you see your best friends? …… (Do you miss them?)**
- **When was the last time you had a good time with your friends? …… (What did you do?)**

Cambridge B2 First: Speaking	Test 3 – Part 2
	4 minutes (6 minutes for groups of three)

1 Couples on holiday	2 College life

Interlocutor In this part of the test, I'm going to give each of you two photographs. I'd like you to talk about your photographs on your own for about a minute, and also to answer a question about your partner's photographs.

(Candidate A), it's your turn first. Here are your photographs. They show **couples enjoying their holidays in different ways**.

*Place **Part 2 Task 1**, in front of Candidate A.*

I'd like you to compare the photographs, and say **what you think they are enjoying about these types of holidays**.

All right?

Candidate A

1 minute

Interlocutor Thank you.

(Candidate B), **what type of holiday would you prefer to go on? …… (Why? / Why not?)**

Candidate B

Approximately 30 seconds

Interlocutor Thank you. (Can I have the booklet, please?) *Retrieve **Part 2 Task 1**.*

Now, *(Candidate B)*, here are your photographs. They show **students in college spending time in different places**.

*Place **Part 2 Task 2**, in front of Candidate B.*

I'd like you to compare the photographs, and say **why you think the students are spending time in these places**.

All right?

Candidate B

1 minute

Interlocutor Thank you.

(Candidate A), **do you prefer to study at home or in a library? …… (Why?)**

Candidate A

Approximately 30 seconds

Interlocutor Thank you. (Can I have the booklet, please?) *Retrieve **Part 2 Task 2**.*

What are the couples enjoying about these types of holidays?

Cambridge B2 First: Speaking

Test 3 – Part 2
Task 2

Why are the students spending time in these places?

Test 3 – Part 3
4 minutes (5 minutes for groups of three)

Cambridge B2 First: Speaking

Choosing an artistic career

Interlocutor	Now, I'd like you to talk about something together for about two minutes *(3 minutes for groups of three)*.
	Here are some artistic careers some people decide to embark on and a question for you to discuss. First you have some time to look at the task.
	*Place **Part 3 Task 3**, in front of the candidates. Allow 15 seconds.*
	Now, talk to each other about **why people decide to embark on these artistic careers**.
Candidate A	

2 minutes (3 minutes for groups of three)

Interlocutor	Thank you. Now you have about a minute to decide **which careers would be the easiest and which would be the most difficult**.
Candidate B	

Approximately 30 seconds

Interlocutor	Thank you. (Can I have the booklet, please?) *Retrieve **Part 3 Task 3**.*

Part 4
4 minutes (6 minutes for groups of three)

Interlocutor *Use the following questions, in order, as appropriate:*

> *Select any of the following prompts, as appropriate:*
> • What do you think?
> • Do you agree?
> • And you?

- Do you think enough people become artists nowadays? …… (Why? / Why not?)
- What do you think are the advantages and disadvantages of becoming an artist nowadays?
- Some people believe that being an artist is not a real job. Do you agree? …… (Why? / Why not?)
- Do you believe schools and universities help people to become artists nowadays? …… (Why? / Why not?)
- In your opinion, should art be as important in schools as other subjects? …… (Why? / Why not?)
- Do you think that people would visit museums more often if they were cheaper or free? …… (Why? / Why not?)

Interlocutor Thank you. That is the end of the test.

Cambridge B2 First: Speaking

Test 3 – Part 3
Task 3

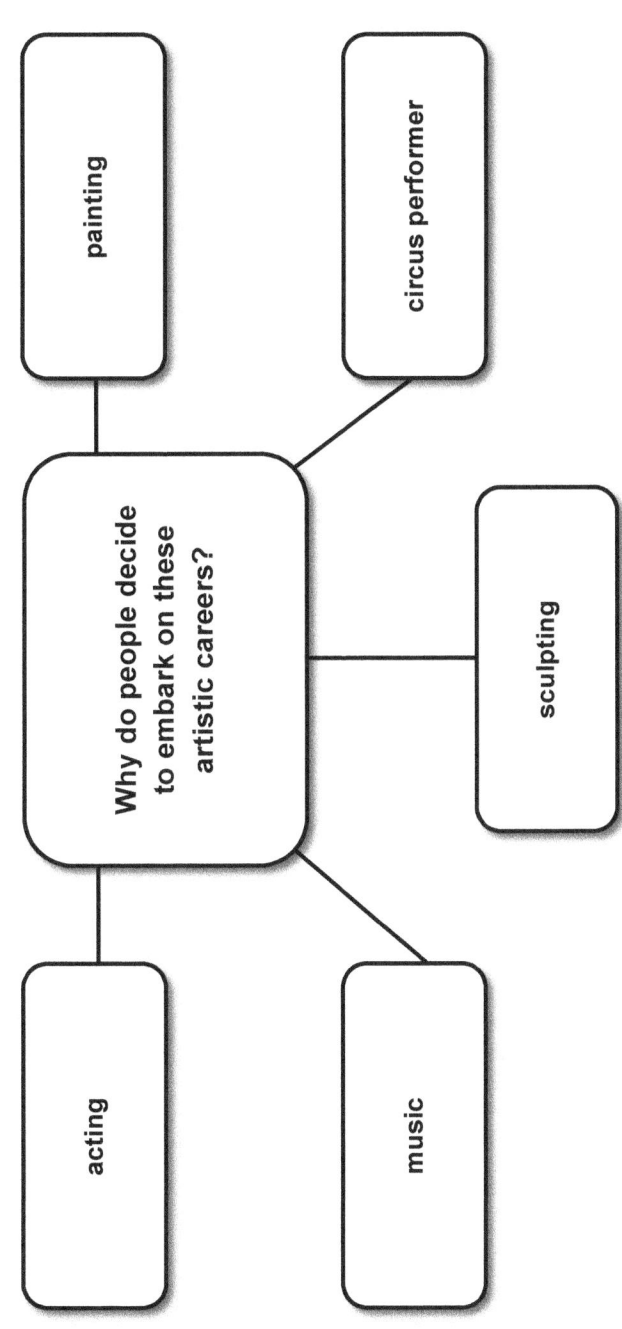

| Mark sheet | Cambridge B2 First: Speaking |

DD	MM	YY

Candidate

Marks awarded

Grammar and vocabulary	0	1	1.5	2	2.5	3	3.5	4	4.5	5
Discourse management	0	1	1.5	2	2.5	3	3.5	4	4.5	5
Pronunciation	0	1	1.5	2	2.5	3	3.5	4	4.5	5
Interactive communication	0	1	1.5	2	2.5	3	3.5	4	4.5	5

Item descriptors

Grammar and vocabulary	• Degree of control of grammatical forms.
	• Range of vocabulary used to give and exchange views.
Discourse management	• Stretches of language produced.
	• Relevance of contributions and organisation of ideas.
	• Use of appropriate cohesive devices and discourse markers.
Pronunciation	• Intelligibility
	• Intonation
	• Word stress
	• Individual sounds
Interactive communication	• Initiating, responding and linking contributions to those of other speakers.
	• Maintaining and developing interaction, and negotiating.

Assessment notes

Cambridge B2 First Speaking

Test 4

Test 4 – Part 1	Cambridge B2 First: Speaking
2 minutes (3 minutes for groups of three)	

Candidates' background

Good morning/afternoon/evening. My name is …………… and this is my colleague …………… .

And your names are?

Can I have your mark sheets, please?

Thank you.

- Where are you from, *(Candidate A)*?
- And you, *(Candidate B)*?

First, we'd like to know something about you.

Select one or more questions from any of the following categories, as appropriate.

Shopping

- **How often do you go shopping for clothes? …… (Why?)**
- **Do ever go shopping with friends or family? …… (Which do you prefer?) …… (Why? / Why not?)**
- **Do you prefer to buy things online or in a physical shop? …… (Why?)**
- **Have you ever had a problem when shopping? …… (Tell us about it.)**

Cooking

- **Who does most of the cooking at home? …… (Why?)**
- **Do you enjoy cooking? …… (Why? / Why not?)**
- **How much time do you spend cooking every day? …… (Why? / Why not?)**
- **Is there a dish you particularly enjoy making? …… (Why do you enjoy it?)**

Employment

- **Do you have a job at present? …… (What do you do?)**
- **Do you think you spend too much time working? …… (Why? / Why not?)**
- **If you could choose, what kind of job would you like to have in the future? …… (Why?)**
- **Is there a job you would really not like to do? …… (What job is it?) …… (Why?)**

Cambridge B2 First: Speaking	Test 4 – Part 2
	4 minutes (6 minutes for groups of three)

1 Reading carefully	2 Spending time outdoors

Interlocutor In this part of the test, I'm going to give each of you two photographs. I'd like you to talk about your photographs on your own for about a minute, and also to answer a question about your partner's photographs.

(Candidate A), it's your turn first. Here are your photographs. They show **people reading something in different situations**.

Place Part 2 Task 1, in front of Candidate A.

I'd like you to compare the photographs, and say **why you think it is important to read carefully in each situation**.

All right?

Candidate A

1 minute

Interlocutor Thank you.

(Candidate B), **what kind of things do you enjoy reading? ...... (Why? / Why not?)**

Candidate B

Approximately 30 seconds

Interlocutor Thank you. (Can I have the booklet, please?) *Retrieve Part 2 Task 1.*

Now, *(Candidate B)*, here are your photographs. They show **people spending their time outdoors for different reasons**.

Place Part 2 Task 2, in front of Candidate B.

I'd like you to compare the photographs, and say **why you think the people might be spending their time outdoors**.

All right?

Candidate B

1 minute

Interlocutor Thank you.

(Candidate A), **do you prefer to spend your free time outdoors or indoors? ...... (Why?)**

Candidate A

Approximately 30 seconds

Interlocutor Thank you. (Can I have the booklet, please?) *Retrieve Part 2 Task 2.*

Cambridge B2 First and FCE are brands belonging to The University of Cambridge and are not associated with Prosperity Education

Test 4 – Part 2
Task 1

Cambridge B2 First: Speaking

Why is it important to read carefully in each situation?

Cambridge B2 First: Speaking

Test 4 – Part 2
Task 2

Why might the people be spending their time outdoors?

Test 4 – Part 3	Cambridge B2 First: Speaking
4 minutes (5 minutes for groups of three)	

Using the internet

Interlocutor	Now, I'd like you to talk about something together for about two minutes *(3 minutes for groups of three)*.
	Here are some ways in which young people use the internet nowadays and a question for you to discuss. First you have some time to look at the task.
	*Place **Part 3 Task 3**, in front of the candidates. Allow 15 seconds.*
	Now, talk to each other about **how young people use the internet nowadays**.
Candidate A	
	....
	2 minutes (3 minutes for groups of three)
Interlocutor	Thank you. Now you have about a minute to decide **the reason why most young people use the internet nowadays**.
Candidate B	
	....
	Approximately 30 seconds
Interlocutor	Thank you. (Can I have the booklet, please?) *Retrieve **Part 3 Task 3**.*

Part 4	
4 minutes (6 minutes for groups of three)	

Interlocutor	*Use the following questions, in order, as appropriate:*	*Select any of the following prompts, as appropriate:*
	• **What do you think are the greatest advantages and disadvantages of using the internet?**	• What do you think? • Do you agree? • And you?
	• **Do you think that young people use the internet in a responsible way?** …… (Why? / Why not?)	
	• **Some people believe that children and teenagers shouldn't be allowed to use the internet on their own. What do you think?** …… (Why? / Why not?)	
	• **Should children be taught how to use the internet at school or at home?** …… (Why? / Why not?)	
	• **Do you think that the internet will ever replace TV or newspapers?** …… (Why? / Why not?)	
	• **In your opinion, is shopping online is a good idea?** …… (Why? / Why not?)	
Interlocutor	Thank you. That is the end of the test.	

Cambridge B2 First: Speaking
Test 4 – Part 3
Task 3

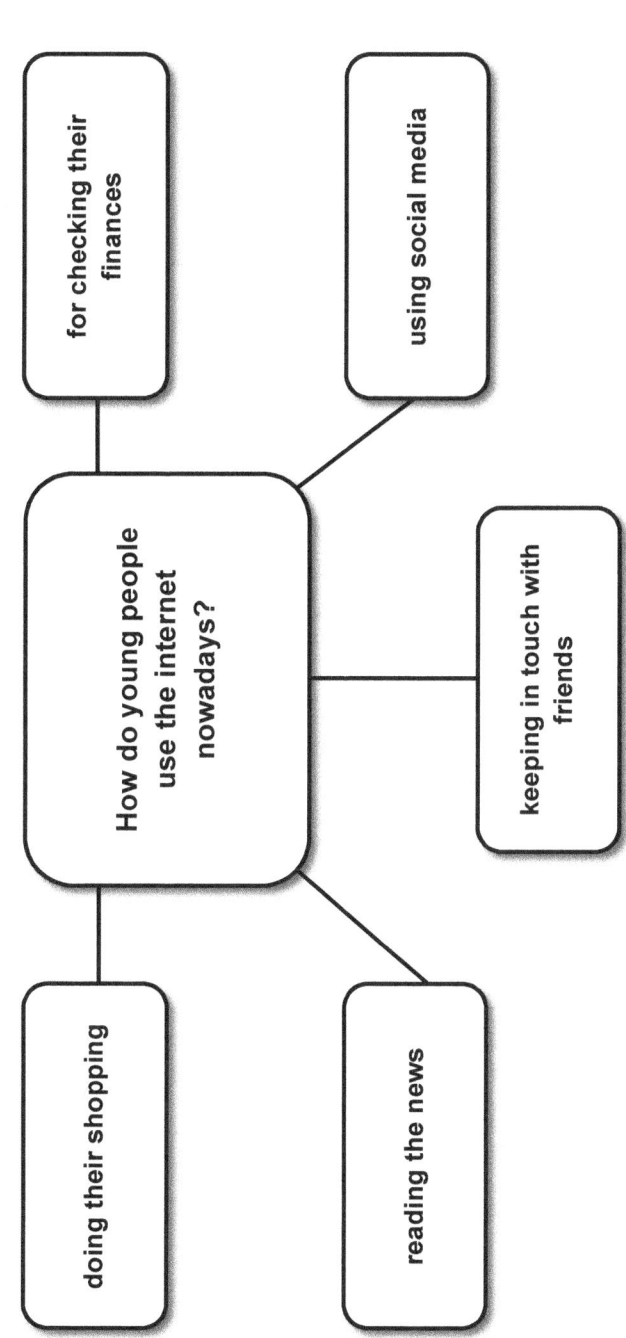

| Mark sheet | Cambridge B2 First: Speaking |

DD	MM	YY

Candidate

Marks awarded

Grammar and vocabulary	0	1	1.5	2	2.5	3	3.5	4	4.5	5
Discourse management	0	1	1.5	2	2.5	3	3.5	4	4.5	5
Pronunciation	0	1	1.5	2	2.5	3	3.5	4	4.5	5
Interactive communication	0	1	1.5	2	2.5	3	3.5	4	4.5	5

Item descriptors

Grammar and vocabulary	• Degree of control of grammatical forms.
	• Range of vocabulary used to give and exchange views.
Discourse management	• Stretches of language produced.
	• Relevance of contributions and organisation of ideas.
	• Use of appropriate cohesive devices and discourse markers.
Pronunciation	• Intelligibility
	• Intonation
	• Word stress
	• Individual sounds
Interactive communication	• Initiating, responding and linking contributions to those of other speakers.
	• Maintaining and developing interaction, and negotiating.

Assessment notes

Cambridge B2 First Speaking

Test 5

Test 5 – Part 1	Cambridge B2 First: Speaking
2 minutes (3 minutes for groups of three)	

Candidates' background

Good morning/afternoon/evening. My name is …………… and this is my colleague …………… .

And your names are?

Can I have your mark sheets, please?

Thank you.

- Where are you from, *(Candidate A)*?
- And you, *(Candidate B)*?

First, we'd like to know something about you.

Select one or more questions from any of the following categories, as appropriate.

Where you live

- **Do you like the area where you live?** …… **(Why? / Why not?)**
- **Is there something you would change about your neighbourhood?** …… **(What is it?)** …… **(Why?)**
- **Do your friends and family live near you?** …… **(Where do they live?)**
- **What's the best way to travel in the area where you live?** …… **(Why?)**

Emails and letters

- **How often do you post letters nowadays?** …… **(Why? / Why not?)**
- **Do you send emails very often?** …… **(Why? / Why not?)**
- **With whom do you normally communicate by email?** …… **(How often?)** …… **(Why?)**
- **Do you think you will send more or fewer emails in the future?** …… **(Why?)**

College / school

- **At the moment, do you go to college or secondary school?** …… **(Tell me more about it)**
- **How long do you spend every day at college/school?** …… **(Why / Why not?)**
- **Is there something you'd like to improve about your college/school?** …… **(What is it?)** …… **(Why?)**
- **Do most of your friends study with you?** …… **(Why? / Why not?)**

Cambridge B2 First: Speaking	Test 5 – Part 2
	4 minutes (6 minutes for groups of three)

1 Working with animals	2 Receiving presents

Interlocutor In this part of the test, I'm going to give each of you two photographs. I'd like you to talk about your photographs on your own for about a minute, and also to answer a question about your partner's photographs.

(Candidate A), it's your turn first. Here are your photographs. They show **people working with animals in different situations**.

Place Part 2 Task 1, in front of Candidate A.

I'd like you to compare the photographs, and say **what you think might be difficult about working with these animals**.

All right?

Candidate A

....

1 minute

Interlocutor Thank you.

(Candidate B), **would you like to have a job working with animals? ...... (Why? / Why not?)**

Candidate B

....

Approximately 30 seconds

Interlocutor Thank you. (Can I have the booklet, please?) *Retrieve Part 2 Task 1.*

Now, *(Candidate B)*, here are your photographs. They show **people receiving presents on different occasions**.

Place Part 2 Task 2, in front of Candidate B.

I'd like you to compare the photographs, and say **why you think the presents might be important for the people who receive them**.

All right?

Candidate B

....

1 minute

Interlocutor Thank you.

(Candidate A), **when was the last time you received a present? ...... (Did you like it?)**

Candidate A

....

Approximately 30 seconds

Interlocutor Thank you. (Can I have the booklet, please?) *Retrieve Part 2 Task 2.*

Cambridge B2 First and FCE are brands belonging to The University of Cambridge and are not associated with Prosperity Education

Test 5 – Part 2
Task 1

Cambridge B2 First: Speaking

What might be difficult about working with these animals?

Cambridge B2 First: Speaking

Test 5 – Part 2
Task 2

Why might the presents be important for the people who receive them?

Test 5 – Part 3
4 minutes (5 minutes for groups of three)

Cambridge B2 First: Speaking

Living abroad

Interlocutor   Now, I'd like you to talk about something together for about two minutes *(3 minutes for groups of three)*.

Here are some reasons why people decide to move abroad and a question for you to discuss. First you have some time to look at the task.

*Place **Part 3 Task 3**, in front of the candidates. Allow 15 seconds.*

Now, talk to each other about **whether it is good for people to decide to move abroad**.

Candidate A

....

2 minutes (3 minutes for groups of three)

Interlocutor   Thank you. Now you have about a minute to decide **what is the best reason for people to move abroad**.

Candidate B

....

Approximately 30 seconds

Interlocutor   Thank you. (Can I have the booklet, please?) *Retrieve **Part 3 Task 3**.*

Part 4
4 minutes (6 minutes for groups of three)

Interlocutor   *Use the following questions, in order, as appropriate:*

> *Select any of the following prompts, as appropriate:*
> • What do you think?
> • Do you agree?
> • And you?

• **Is it possible to learn a new language without travelling abroad?** ...... (Why? / Why not?)

• **Do many foreigners decide to live in your country?** ...... (Why do you think that is?)

• **In recent years, foreign travel has become extremely popular. Do you think this is a good thing?** ...... (Why? / Why not?)

• **Do you think that tourism has more advantages than disadvantages?** ...... (Why?)

• **How do you think the way we travel might change in the future?** ...... (Why? / Why not?)

• **Many people believe that their own country is the best place to live. What do you think?** ...... (Why? / Why not?)

Interlocutor   Thank you. That is the end of the test.

Cambridge B2 First: Speaking
Test 5 – Part 3
Task 3

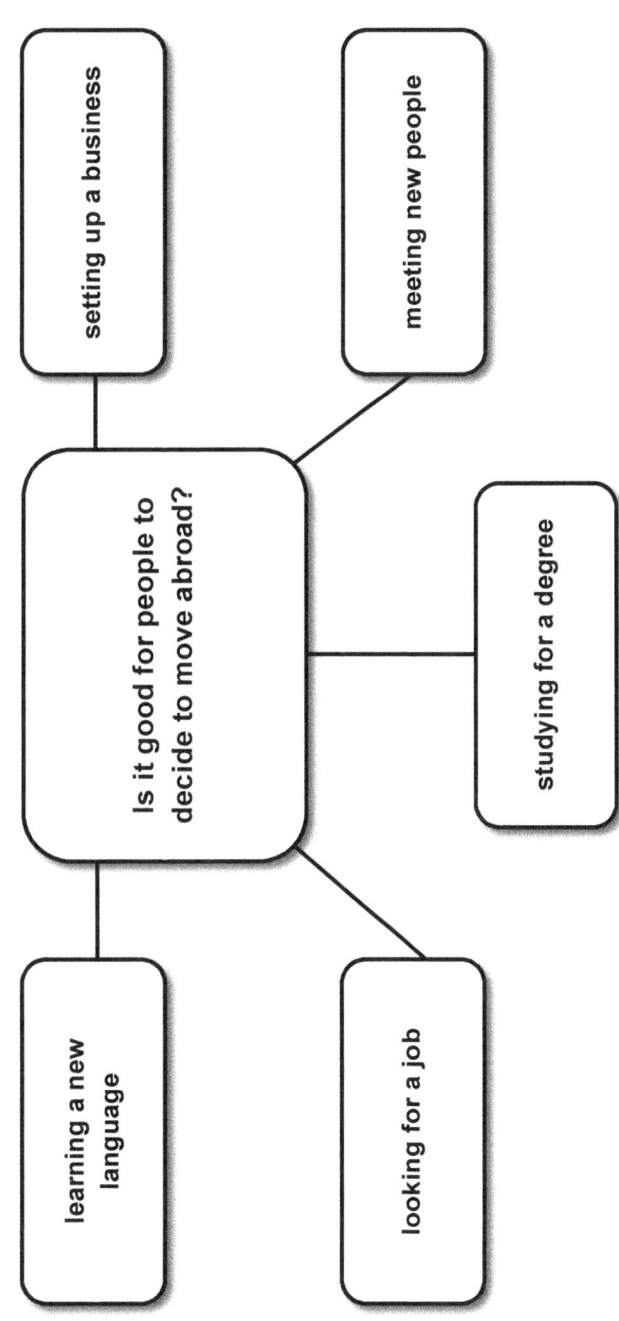

| Mark sheet | Cambridge B2 First: Speaking |

DD	MM	YY

Candidate	

Marks awarded

Grammar and vocabulary	0	1	1.5	2	2.5	3	3.5	4	4.5	5
Discourse management	0	1	1.5	2	2.5	3	3.5	4	4.5	5
Pronunciation	0	1	1.5	2	2.5	3	3.5	4	4.5	5
Interactive communication	0	1	1.5	2	2.5	3	3.5	4	4.5	5

Item descriptors

Grammar and vocabulary	• Degree of control of grammatical forms.
	• Range of vocabulary used to give and exchange views.
Discourse management	• Stretches of language produced.
	• Relevance of contributions and organisation of ideas.
	• Use of appropriate cohesive devices and discourse markers.
Pronunciation	• Intelligibility
	• Intonation
	• Word stress
	• Individual sounds
Interactive communication	• Initiating, responding and linking contributions to those of other speakers.
	• Maintaining and developing interaction, and negotiating.

Assessment notes

Cambridge B2 First Speaking

Test 6

Test 6 – Part 1	Cambridge B2 First: Speaking
2 minutes (3 minutes for groups of three)	

Candidates' background

Good morning/afternoon/evening. My name is .... and this is my colleague ....

And your names are?

Can I have your mark sheets, please?

Thank you.

- Where are you from, *(Candidate A)*?
- And you, *(Candidate B)*?

First, we'd like to know something about you.

Select one or more questions from any of the following categories, as appropriate.

Animals and pets

- Do you like animals in general? …… (Why? / Why not?)
- Are you afraid of any animals in particular? …… (Which ones?)
- Have you got any pets? …… (What pet do you have?) …… (Why not?)
- What's the most popular pet in your country? …… (Why do you think that is?)

Healthy habits

- Is it important for you to keep healthy? …… (Why? / Why not?)
- What have you done in the past to keep healthy? …… (Tell us more about it.)
- Do most people in your country have a healthy diet? …… (Why? / Why not?)
- Is there something you could do to be healthier? …… (What is it?)

Keeping in touch

- Do you live near your best friends? …… (Where do they live?)
- How do you keep in touch with your friends and family?
- How often do you text the people who are close to you? …… (Is that enough in your opinion?)
- Is texting the best way to keep in touch with people? …… (Why? / Why not?)

Cambridge B2 First and FCE are brands belonging to The University of Cambridge and are not associated with Prosperity Education

Cambridge B2 First: Speaking	Test 6 – Part 2
	4 minutes (6 minutes for groups of three)

1 Waiting patiently	2 Professionals discussing

Interlocutor In this part of the test, I'm going to give each of you two photographs. I'd like you to talk about your photographs on your own for about a minute, and also to answer a question about your partner's photographs.

(Candidate A), it's your turn first. Here are your photographs. They show **people waiting for something in different places**.

*Place **Part 2 Task 1**, in front of Candidate A.*

I'd like you to compare the photographs, and say **why you think it might be important to keep calm in these situations**.

All right?

Candidate A

1 minute

Interlocutor Thank you.

(Candidate B), **in which situation would you get most nervous? ...... (Why? / Why not?)**

Candidate B

Approximately 30 seconds

Interlocutor Thank you. (Can I have the booklet, please?) *Retrieve **Part 2 Task 1**.*

Now, *(Candidate B)*, here are your photographs. They show **teams of professionals discussing something at work**.

*Place **Part 2 Task 2**, in front of Candidate B.*

I'd like you to compare the photographs, and say **what you think they might be discussing**.

All right?

Candidate B

1 minute

Interlocutor Thank you.

(Candidate A), **in which situation do you think the discussion is more important? ...... (Why?)**

Candidate A

Approximately 30 seconds

Interlocutor Thank you. (Can I have the booklet, please?) *Retrieve **Part 2 Task 2**.*

Test 6 – Part 2
Task 1

Cambridge B2 First: Speaking

Why might it be important to keep calm in these situations?

Cambridge B2 First: Speaking

Test 6 – Part 2
Task 2

What might the teams be discussing?

Test 6 – Part 3	Cambridge B2 First: Speaking
4 minutes (5 minutes for groups of three)	

Taking care of the environment

Interlocutor	Now, I'd like you to talk about something together for about two minutes *(3 minutes for groups of three)*.
	Here are some things we can do to take care of the environment and a question for you to discuss. First you have some time to look at the task.
	*Place **Part 3 Task 3**, in front of the candidates. Allow 15 seconds.*
	Now, talk to each other about **how effective these ideas are when taking care of the environment**.

Candidate A

2 minutes (3 minutes for groups of three)

Interlocutor	Thank you. Now you have about a minute to decide **which idea is the easiest to put into practice in your everyday life**.

Candidate B

Approximately 30 seconds

Interlocutor	Thank you. (Can I have the booklet, please?) *Retrieve **Part 3 Task 3**.*

Part 4
4 minutes (6 minutes for groups of three)

Interlocutor	*Use the following questions, in order, as appropriate:*	*Select any of the following prompts, as appropriate:*
	• **Is there anything else we can do to look after the environment?** …… (What is it?)	• What do you think? • Do you agree? • And you?
	• **Do you think that people in your country do enough to protect the environment?** …… (Why? / Why not?)	
	• **In your opinion, who should do more to protect the environment: citizens or governments?** …… (Why? / Why not?)	
	• **Some people believe global warming is not a real problem. What do you think?** …… (Why? / Why not?)	
	• **Many people believe that it's too late to save the environment. Do you agree?** …… (Why? / Why not?)	
	• **Should teachers be responsible for teaching children to recycle?** …… (Why? / Why not?)	

Interlocutor	Thank you. That is the end of the test.

Cambridge B2 First and FCE are brands belonging to The University of Cambridge and are not associated with Prosperity Education

Cambridge B2 First: Speaking

Test 6 – Part 3
Task 3

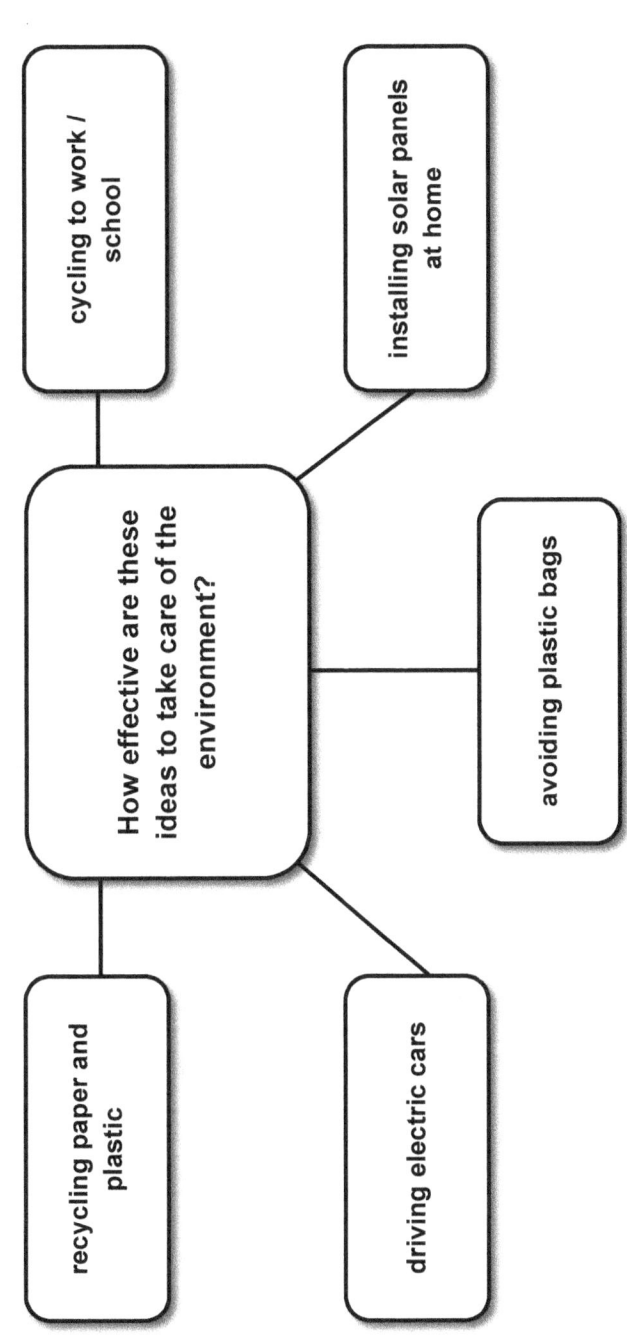

Mark sheet	Cambridge B2 First: Speaking

DD	MM	YY

Candidate	

Marks awarded

Grammar and vocabulary	0	1	1.5	2	2.5	3	3.5	4	4.5	5
Discourse management	0	1	1.5	2	2.5	3	3.5	4	4.5	5
Pronunciation	0	1	1.5	2	2.5	3	3.5	4	4.5	5
Interactive communication	0	1	1.5	2	2.5	3	3.5	4	4.5	5

Item descriptors

Grammar and vocabulary	• Degree of control of grammatical forms.
	• Range of vocabulary used to give and exchange views.
Discourse management	• Stretches of language produced.
	• Relevance of contributions and organisation of ideas.
	• Use of appropriate cohesive devices and discourse markers.
Pronunciation	• Intelligibility
	• Intonation
	• Word stress
	• Individual sounds
Interactive communication	• Initiating, responding and linking contributions to those of other speakers.
	• Maintaining and developing interaction, and negotiating.

Assessment notes

Cambridge B2 First Speaking

Test 7

Test 7 – Part 1	Cambridge B2 First: Speaking
2 minutes (3 minutes for groups of three)	

Candidates' background

Good morning/afternoon/evening. My name is …………… and this is my colleague …………… .

And your names are?

Can I have your mark sheets, please?

Thank you.

- Where are you from, *(Candidate A)*?
- And you, *(Candidate B)*?

First, we'd like to know something about you.

Select one or more questions from any of the following categories, as appropriate.

Journeys

- **How did you get here today?** …… **(Did you drive here?)** …… **(Why?)**
- **Is there a journey you often make?** …… **(What's it like?)**
- **How regularly do you take the bus/train?** …… **(Why? / Why not?)**
- **What's the best way to move around the area where you live?**

Arts

- **Are you an artistic person?** …… **(Why? / Why not?)**
- **Did/do you study arts in school?** …… **(Why? / Why not?)**
- **If you could, would you like to work as an artist?** …… **(Why? / Why not?)**
- **Are there any artists in your country that you admire?** …… **(Why do you admire them?)**

Computers

- **Do you own any electronic devices?** …… **(Which one(s)?)** …… **(Why not?)**
- **How often do you use a computer?** …… **(Why? / Why not?)**
- **What do you normally use computers for?**
- **Are computers useful if you don't have an internet connection?** …… **(Why? / Why not?)**

Cambridge B2 First: Speaking	Test 7 – Part 2
	4 minutes (6 minutes for groups of three)

1 Trying to concentrate	2 Doing the shopping

Interlocutor In this part of the test, I'm going to give each of you two photographs. I'd like you to talk about your photographs on your own for about a minute, and also to answer a question about your partner's photographs.

(Candidate A), it's your turn first. Here are your photographs. They show **people trying to concentrate while doing different activities**.

*Place **Part 2 Task 1**, in front of Candidate A.*

I'd like you to compare the photographs, and say **how difficult you think it is for the people to concentrate in these situations**.

All right?

Candidate A

1 minute

Interlocutor Thank you.

(Candidate B), **do you find it easy to concentrate when you're studying? ...... (Why?)**

Candidate B

Approximately 30 seconds

Interlocutor Thank you. (Can I have the booklet, please?) *Retrieve **Part 2 Task 1**.*

Now, *(Candidate B)*, here are your photographs. They show **people doing their shopping in different places**.

*Place **Part 2 Task 2**, in front of Candidate B.*

I'd like you to compare the photographs, and say **why you think the people have decided to do their shopping in these places**.

All right?

Candidate B

1 minute

Interlocutor Thank you.

(Candidate A), **in which of these places would you prefer to do your shopping? ...... (Why?)**

Candidate A

Approximately 30 seconds

Interlocutor Thank you. (Can I have the booklet, please?) *Retrieve **Part 2 Task 2**.*

Cambridge B2 First and FCE are brands belonging to The University of Cambridge and are not associated with Prosperity Education

Test 7 – Part 2
Task 1

Cambridge B2 First: Speaking

How difficult is it for the people to concentrate in these situations?

Cambridge B2 First: Speaking

Test 7 – Part 2
Task 2

Why have the people decided to do their shopping in these places?

Test 7 – Part 3	Cambridge B2 First: Speaking
4 minutes (5 minutes for groups of three)	

Improving life in the city

Interlocutor Now, I'd like you to talk about something together for about two minutes *(3 minutes for groups of three)*.

Some people say cities should try to attract tourists, but other people disagree. Here are some things that can be done to improve life in a city and a question for you to discuss. First you have some time to look at the task.

*Place **Part 3 Task 3**, in front of the candidates. Allow 15 seconds.*

Now, talk to each other about **whether these things would attract more tourists or improve life for the locals**.

Candidate A

....

2 minutes (3 minutes for groups of three)

Interlocutor Thank you. Now you have about a minute to decide **which change would benefit both tourists and locals the most**.

Candidate B

....

Approximately 30 seconds

Interlocutor Thank you. (Can I have the booklet, please?) *Retrieve **Part 3 Task 3**.*

Part 4
4 minutes (6 minutes for groups of three)

Interlocutor *Use the following questions, in order, as appropriate:*

- What other things can cities do to attract more visitors?

- Do you think that visitors can have a negative impact on a city? ...... (Why? / Why not?)

- What are the main advantages and disadvantages of living in a big city?

- Some people believe that building cycling lanes in cities is the best way to fight air pollution. Do you agree? ...... (Why? / Why not?)

- Is there an important change that you would like to see in the area where you live? ...... (What is it?) ...... (Why? / Why not?)

- Some people believe that parks and green spaces are important for life in the city. What do you think? ...... (Why?)

Select any of the following prompts, as appropriate:

- What do you think?
- Do you agree?
- And you?

Interlocutor Thank you. That is the end of the test.

Cambridge B2 First and FCE are brands belonging to The University of Cambridge and are not associated with Prosperity Education

Cambridge B2 First: Speaking

Test 7 – Part 3
Task 3

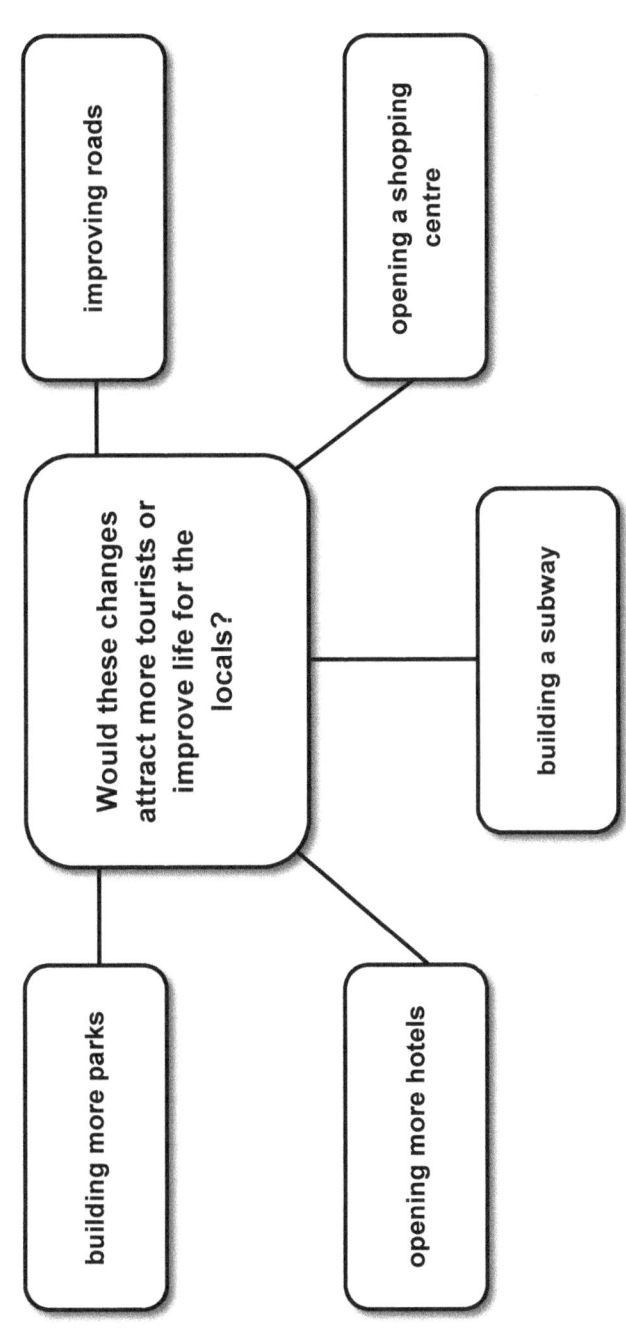

| Mark sheet | Cambridge B2 First: Speaking |

DD	MM	YY

Candidate	

Marks awarded

Grammar and vocabulary	0	1	1.5	2	2.5	3	3.5	4	4.5	5
Discourse management	0	1	1.5	2	2.5	3	3.5	4	4.5	5
Pronunciation	0	1	1.5	2	2.5	3	3.5	4	4.5	5
Interactive communication	0	1	1.5	2	2.5	3	3.5	4	4.5	5

Item descriptors

Grammar and vocabulary	• Degree of control of grammatical forms.
	• Range of vocabulary used to give and exchange views.
Discourse management	• Stretches of language produced.
	• Relevance of contributions and organisation of ideas.
	• Use of appropriate cohesive devices and discourse markers.
Pronunciation	• Intelligibility
	• Intonation
	• Word stress
	• Individual sounds
Interactive communication	• Initiating, responding and linking contributions to those of other speakers.
	• Maintaining and developing interaction, and negotiating.

Assessment notes

Cambridge B2 First Speaking

Test 8

Test 8 – Part 1	Cambridge B2 First: Speaking
2 minutes (3 minutes for groups of three)	

Candidates' background

Good morning/afternoon/evening. My name is …………… and this is my colleague …………… .

And your names are?

Can I have your mark sheets, please?

Thank you.

- Where are you from, *(Candidate A)*?
- And you, *(Candidate B)*?

First, we'd like to know something about you.

Select one or more questions from any of the following categories, as appropriate.

Flying

- **Are you afraid of flying? …… (Why? / Why not?)**
- **Have you ever had a bad flight? …… (Tell us about it.)**
- **When was the last time you travelled by plane? …… (Where did you go?)**
- **Which do you prefer: travelling by plane or by train? …… (Why?)**

Travelling abroad

- **What do you like to do when you're on holiday? …… (Why?)**
- **Do you enjoy travelling abroad, or do you prefer to stay in your own country? …… (Why?)**
- **What's the best thing about your country for tourists? …… (Why?)**
- **When you travel abroad, what kind of accommodation do you book? …… (What's good about it?)**

Advice

- **Are you good at giving advice? …… (Why? / Why not?)**
- **When was the last time you gave advice to someone? …… (Tell us about it.)**
- **In what situations do you ask for advice? …… (Why? / Why not?)**
- **Who do you ask for advice when you need it? …… (Why?)**

Cambridge B2 First: Speaking	Test 8 – Part 2
	4 minutes (6 minutes for groups of three)

1 Learning in different ways	2 Means of transport

Interlocutor In this part of the test, I'm going to give each of you two photographs. I'd like you to talk about your photographs on your own for about a minute, and also to answer a question about your partner's photographs.

(Candidate A), it's your turn first. Here are your photographs. They show **people learning in different ways**.

Place **Part 2 Task 1**, *in front of Candidate A*.

I'd like you to compare the photographs, and say **what you think the advantages are of learning in these ways**.

All right?

Candidate A

1 minute

Interlocutor Thank you.

(Candidate B), **how would you prefer to learn a new language? …… (Why?)**

Candidate B

Approximately 30 seconds

Interlocutor Thank you. (Can I have the booklet, please?) *Retrieve Part 2 Task 1.*

Now, *(Candidate B)*, here are your photographs. They show **people travelling to work using different means of transport**.

Place **Part 2** booklet, *open at Task 2, in front of Candidate B*.

I'd like you to compare the photographs, and say **why you think the people have decided to use these means of transport**.

All right?

Candidate B

1 minute

Interlocutor Thank you.

(Candidate A), **do you use public transport regularly? …… (Why? / Why not?)**

Candidate A

Approximately 30 seconds

Interlocutor Thank you. (Can I have the booklet, please?) *Retrieve Part 2 Task 2.*

Cambridge B2 First and FCE are brands belonging to The University of Cambridge and are not associated with Prosperity Education

Test 8 – Part 2
Task 1

Cambridge B2 First: Speaking

What are the advantages of learning in these ways?

Why have the people decided to use these means of transport?

Test 8 – Part 3	Cambridge B2 First: Speaking
4 minutes (5 minutes for groups of three)	

Improving a local college

Interlocutor Now, I'd like you to talk about something together for about two minutes *(3 minutes for groups of three)*.

I'd like you to imagine that a local college has money to improve their facilities. Here are some things they can spend their money on and a question for you to discuss. First you have some time to look at the task.

*Place **Part 3 Task 3**, in front of the candidates. Allow 15 seconds.*

Now, talk to each other about **how these things would improve the local college for students**.

Candidate A

2 minutes (3 minutes for groups of three)

Interlocutor Thank you. Now you have about a minute to decide **which two things the college should invest the money in**.

Candidate B

Approximately 30 seconds

Interlocutor Thank you. (Can I have the booklet, please?) *Retrieve **Part 3 Task 3**.*

Part 4
4 minutes (6 minutes for groups of three)

Interlocutor *Use the following questions, in order, as appropriate:*

- Do you think studying at university should be free for everyone? ...... (Why? / Why not?)

- Is there anything you would change about universities in your country? ...... (Why?)

- Some people believe that everyone should study at university. Do you agree? ...... (Why? / Why not?)

- Do you think young people should study what their parents want them to study? ...... (Why? / Why not?)

- Nowadays it is very popular to study for a year abroad. Do you think this is a good idea? ...... (Why? / Why not?)

- How can students benefit from taking a gap year before studying?

Select any of the following prompts, as appropriate:
- What do you think?
- Do you agree?
- And you?

Interlocutor Thank you. That is the end of the test.

Cambridge B2 First and FCE are brands belonging to The University of Cambridge and are not associated with Prosperity Education

Cambridge B2 First: Speaking

Test 8 – Part 3
Task 3

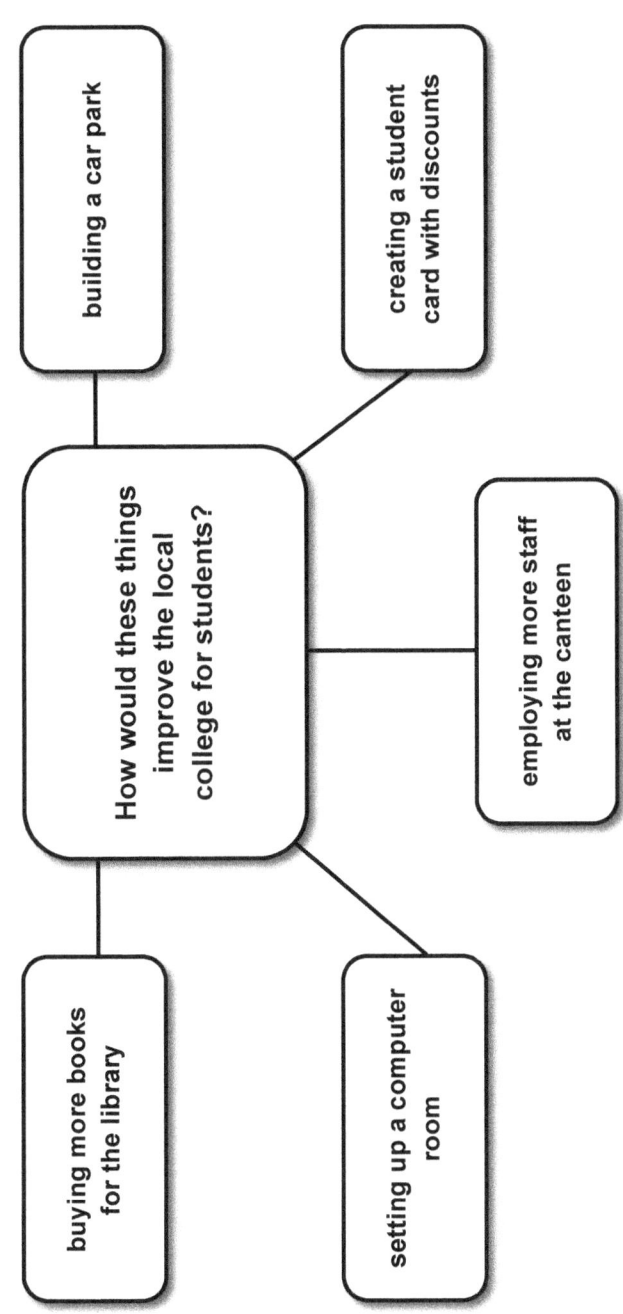

Mark sheet   Cambridge B2 First: Speaking

DD	MM	YY

Candidate:

Marks awarded

Grammar and vocabulary	0	1	1.5	2	2.5	3	3.5	4	4.5	5
Discourse management	0	1	1.5	2	2.5	3	3.5	4	4.5	5
Pronunciation	0	1	1.5	2	2.5	3	3.5	4	4.5	5
Interactive communication	0	1	1.5	2	2.5	3	3.5	4	4.5	5

Item descriptors

Grammar and vocabulary	• Degree of control of grammatical forms.
	• Range of vocabulary used to give and exchange views.
Discourse management	• Stretches of language produced.
	• Relevance of contributions and organisation of ideas.
	• Use of appropriate cohesive devices and discourse markers.
Pronunciation	• Intelligibility
	• Intonation
	• Word stress
	• Individual sounds
Interactive communication	• Initiating, responding and linking contributions to those of other speakers.
	• Maintaining and developing interaction, and negotiating.

Assessment notes

Cambridge B2 First Speaking

Test 9

Test 9 – Part 1	Cambridge B2 First: Speaking
2 minutes (3 minutes for groups of three)	

Candidates' background

Good morning/afternoon/evening. My name is .... and this is my colleague ....

And your names are?

Can I have your mark sheets, please?

Thank you.

- Where are you from, *(Candidate A)*?
- And you, *(Candidate B)*?

First, we'd like to know something about you.

Select one or more questions from any of the following categories, as appropriate.

Celebrities

- **What kind of celebrities are most famous in your country? ...... (What are they famous for?)**
- **Do you admire any national or international celebrities? ...... (Why? / Why not?)**
- **Would you like to become a celebrity one day? ...... (Why? / Why not?)**
- **Is there something you would like to become famous for? ...... (What is it?) (Why not?)**

Extreme sports

- **Do you do any extreme sports? ...... (Why? / Why not?)**
- **Have you ever had an injury while doing sport? ...... (What happened?)**
- **Would you like to try any dangerous sports in the future? ...... (Why? / Why not?)**
- **If you could, would you warn people against doing some extreme sports? ...... (Why? / Why not?)**

Money and jobs

- **Do you live in an expensive area? ...... (Why? / Why not?)**
- **Is money important to you? ...... (Why? / Why not?)**
- **Would you like to have a job with a high salary? ...... (Why? / Why not?)**
- **What's more important to you: having money or free time? ...... (Why?)**

Cambridge B2 First: Speaking	Test 9 – Part 2
	4 minutes (6 minutes for groups of three)

1 Taking a break	2 Using electronic devices

Interlocutor In this part of the test, I'm going to give each of you two photographs. I'd like you to talk about your photographs on your own for about a minute, and also to answer a question about your partner's photographs.

(Candidate A), it's your turn first. Here are your photographs. They show **people taking a break in different situations**.

Place Part 2 Task 1, in front of Candidate A.

I'd like you to compare the photographs, and say **why you think it might be important for these people to take a break**.

All right?

Candidate A

....

1 minute

Interlocutor Thank you.

(Candidate B), **when do you need to take a break? …… (Why? / Why not?)**

Candidate B

....

Approximately 30 seconds

Interlocutor Thank you. (Can I have the booklet, please?) *Retrieve Part 2 Task 1.*

Now, *(Candidate B)*, here are your photographs. They show **people using electronic devices in different situations**.

Place Part 2 booklet, open at Task 2, in front of Candidate B.

I'd like you to compare the photographs, and say **why you think the people have chosen to use these electronic devices**.

All right?

Candidate B

....

1 minute

Interlocutor Thank you.

(Candidate A), **which electronic devices do you use every day? …… (Why?)**

Candidate A

....

Approximately 30 seconds

Interlocutor Thank you. (Can I have the booklet, please?) *Retrieve Part 2 Task 2.*

Cambridge B2 First and FCE are brands belonging to The University of Cambridge and are not associated with Prosperity Education

Test 9 – Part 2
Task 1

Cambridge B2 First: Speaking

Why might it be important for these people to take a break?

Why have the people chosen to use these electronic devices?

Test 9 – Part 3	Cambridge B2 First: Speaking
4 minutes (5 minutes for groups of three)	

Reducing traffic in cities

Interlocutor Now, I'd like you to talk about something together for about two minutes *(3 minutes for groups of three)*.

Here are some measures countries can take to reduce traffic in their cities and a question for you to discuss. First you have some time to look at the task.

*Place **Part 3 Task 3**, in front of the candidates. Allow 15 seconds.*

Now, talk to each other about **how these measures can help to reduce traffic in cities**.

Candidate A

....

2 minutes (3 minutes for groups of three)

Interlocutor Thank you. Now you have about a minute to decide **which measure would be the most effective in the long term**.

Candidate B

....

Approximately 30 seconds

Interlocutor Thank you. (Can I have the booklet, please?) *Retrieve **Part 3 Task 3**.*

Part 4
4 minutes (6 minutes for groups of three)

Interlocutor *Use the following questions, in order, as appropriate:*

- In your opinion, what can people do to reduce traffic in big cities? ...... (Is this easy to achieve?)

- Is traffic a big problem in the area where you live? ...... (Why? / Why not?)

- Some people say that driving is the best way to travel. Do you agree? ...... (Why? / Why not?)

- What would be the advantages and disadvantages of <u>not</u> owning a car?

- Some people believe that cars and petrol are responsible for global warming. What do you think? ...... (Why? / Why not?)

- In the future, do you believe people will drive more or less than now? ...... (Why?)

Select any of the following prompts, as appropriate:
- What do you think?
- Do you agree?
- And you?

Interlocutor Thank you. That is the end of the test.

Cambridge B2 First: Speaking

Test 9 – Part 3
Task 3

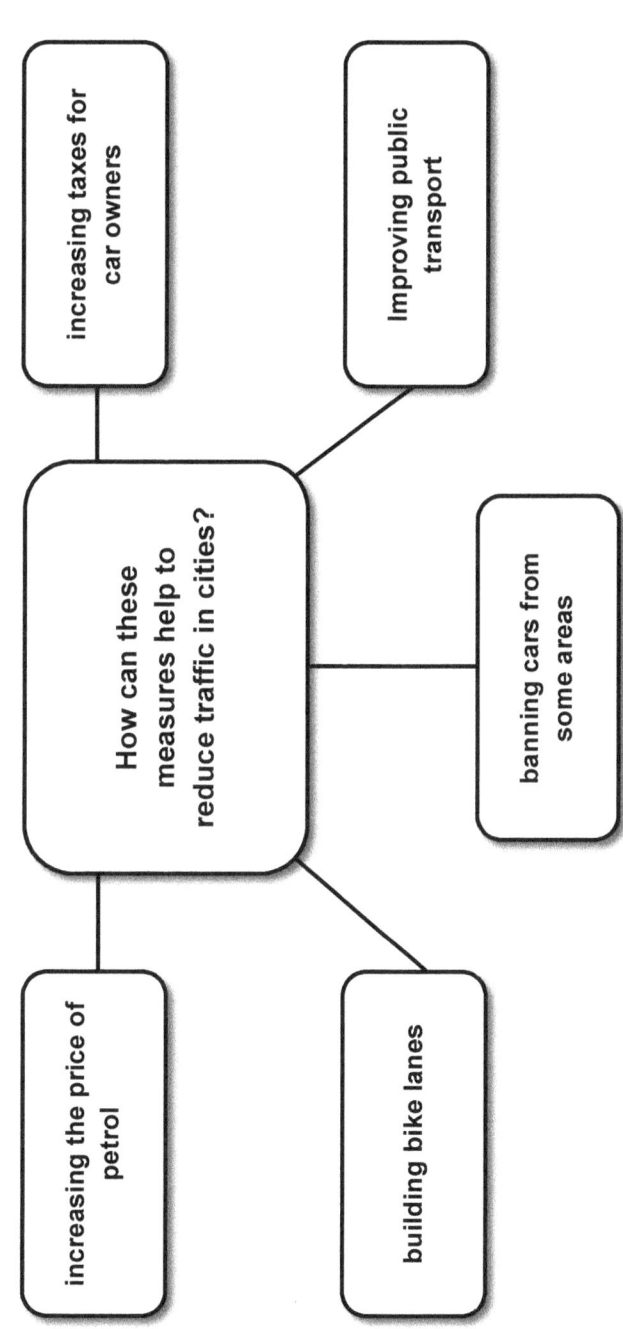

Mark sheet			Cambridge B2 First: Speaking

DD	MM	YY

Candidate	

Marks awarded

Grammar and vocabulary	0	1	1.5	2	2.5	3	3.5	4	4.5	5
Discourse management	0	1	1.5	2	2.5	3	3.5	4	4.5	5
Pronunciation	0	1	1.5	2	2.5	3	3.5	4	4.5	5
Interactive communication	0	1	1.5	2	2.5	3	3.5	4	4.5	5

Item descriptors

Grammar and vocabulary	• Degree of control of grammatical forms. • Range of vocabulary used to give and exchange views.
Discourse management	• Stretches of language produced. • Relevance of contributions and organisation of ideas. • Use of appropriate cohesive devices and discourse markers.
Pronunciation	• Intelligibility • Intonation • Word stress • Individual sounds
Interactive communication	• Initiating, responding and linking contributions to those of other speakers. • Maintaining and developing interaction, and negotiating.

Assessment notes

Cambridge B2 First Speaking

Test 10

Test 10 – Part 1	Cambridge B2 First: Speaking
2 minutes (3 minutes for groups of three)	

Candidates' background

Good morning/afternoon/evening. My name is ………….. and this is my colleague ………….. .

And your names are?

Can I have your mark sheets, please?

Thank you.

- Where are you from, *(Candidate A)*?
- And you, *(Candidate B)*?

First, we'd like to know something about you.

Select one or more questions from any of the following categories, as appropriate.

Adventure activities

- **Are you an adventurous person? …… (Why? / Why not?)**
- **Have you ever been on an adventure holiday? …… (Why? / Why not?)**
- **Do you enjoy doing extreme sports like climbing? …… (Why? / Why not?)**
- **Is there an adventure sport you'd like to do in the future? …… (Why? / Why not?)**

Being at home

- **Do you live in a house or an apartment? …… (Do you like it?) …… (Why? / Why not?)**
- **Have you always lived in the same house/apartment? …… (Why? / Why not?)**
- **How much time do you spend at home every day? …… (Do you think it's enough?) …… (Why?)**
- **What do you like to do when you're at home? …… (Why? / Why not?)**

Languages

- **How long have you been learning English? …… (When did you start?)**
- **Will English be useful to you in the future? …… (How?) …… (Why? / Why not?)**
- **Do you speak any other languages? …… (Which one(s)?) …… (How did you learn it/them?)**
- **If you had the time, which other languages would you like to learn? …… (Why?)**

Cambridge B2 First: Speaking	Test 10 – Part 2
	4 minutes (6 minutes for groups of three)

1 Spending the weekend	2 Taking pictures

Interlocutor In this part of the test, I'm going to give each of you two photographs. I'd like you to talk about your photographs on your own for about a minute, and also to answer a question about your partner's photographs.

(Candidate A), it's your turn first. Here are your photographs. They show **people spending their weekends in different places**.

*Place **Part 2 Task 1**, in front of Candidate A.*

I'd like you to compare the photographs, and say **why you think the people have decided to spend their weekend in these places**.

All right?

Candidate A

1 minute

Interlocutor Thank you.

(Candidate B), **where would you prefer to spend your weekend? …… (Why?)**

Candidate B

Approximately 30 seconds

Interlocutor Thank you. (Can I have the booklet, please?) *Retrieve **Part 2 Task 1**.*

Now, *(Candidate B)*, here are your photographs. They show **people taking pictures of different things**.

*Place **Part 2** booklet, open at **Task 2**, in front of Candidate B.*

I'd like you to compare the photographs, and say **what you think the people will do with the pictures after taking them**.

All right?

Candidate B

1 minute

Interlocutor Thank you.

(Candidate A), **do you normally take pictures of your food? …… (Why? / Why not?)**

Candidate A

Approximately 30 seconds

Interlocutor Thank you. (Can I have the booklet, please?) *Retrieve **Part 2 Task 2**.*

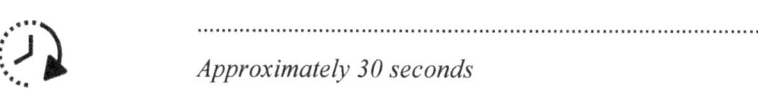

Test 10 – Part 2
Task 1

Cambridge B2 First: Speaking

Why have the people decided to spend their weekend in these places?

Cambridge B2 First: Speaking

Test 10 – Part 2
Task 2

What will the people do with the pictures after taking them?

Test 10 – Part 3	Cambridge B2 First: Speaking
4 minutes (5 minutes for groups of three)	

Young people earning money

Interlocutor Now, I'd like you to talk about something together for about two minutes *(3 minutes for groups of three)*.

Some people believe that students should have a part-time job, but other people disagree. Here are some advantages and disadvantages of students having a part-time job and a question for you to discuss. First you have some time to look at the task.

*Place **Part 3 Task 3**, in front of the candidates. Allow 15 seconds.*

Now, talk to each other about **whether students should have a part-time job or not**.

Candidate A

2 minutes (3 minutes for groups of three)

Interlocutor Thank you. Now you have about a minute to decide **what the best reason is to have a job when you are a student**.

Candidate B

Approximately 30 seconds

Interlocutor Thank you. (Can I have the booklet, please?) *Retrieve **Part 3 Task 3**.*

Part 4
4 minutes (6 minutes for groups of three)

Interlocutor *Use the following questions, in order, as appropriate:*

- Do you think it is a good idea to have a job while you're in college? …… (Why? / Why not?)
- Do most young people in your country have a job while they are studying? …… (Why? / Why not?)
- Some people prefer to have one job their whole life instead of several different jobs. What about you? …… (Why?)
- Would you like to have a job that pays well even if you don't have much free time? …… (Why? / Why not?)
- Do you think that working from home is a good idea? …… (Why? / Why not?)
- In general, how do you think employers can make their employees happier?

Select any of the following prompts, as appropriate:
- What do you think?
- Do you agree?
- And you?

Interlocutor Thank you. That is the end of the test.

Cambridge B2 First and FCE are brands belonging to The University of Cambridge and are not associated with Prosperity Education

Cambridge B2 First: Speaking

Test 10 – Part 3 — Task 3

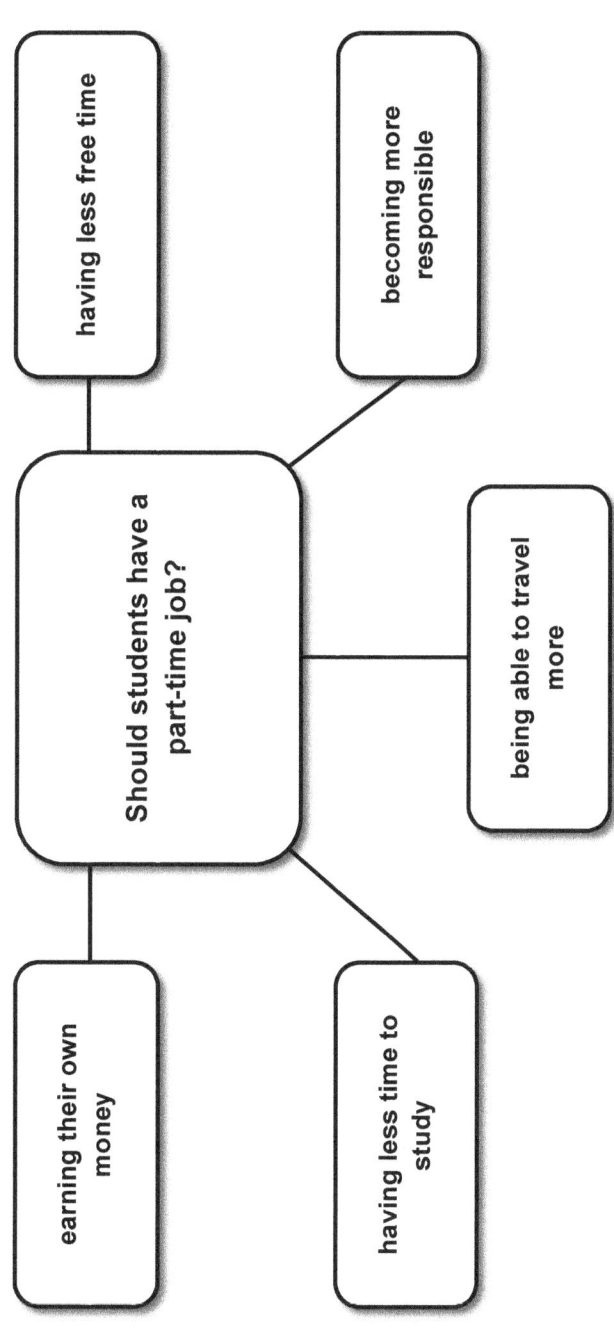

| Mark sheet | Cambridge B2 First: Speaking |

DD	MM	YY

Candidate	

Marks awarded

Grammar and vocabulary	0	1	1.5	2	2.5	3	3.5	4	4.5	5
Discourse management	0	1	1.5	2	2.5	3	3.5	4	4.5	5
Pronunciation	0	1	1.5	2	2.5	3	3.5	4	4.5	5
Interactive communication	0	1	1.5	2	2.5	3	3.5	4	4.5	5

Item descriptors

Grammar and vocabulary	• Degree of control of grammatical forms.
	• Range of vocabulary used to give and exchange views.
Discourse management	• Stretches of language produced.
	• Relevance of contributions and organisation of ideas.
	• Use of appropriate cohesive devices and discourse markers.
Pronunciation	• Intelligibility
	• Intonation
	• Word stress
	• Individual sounds
Interactive communication	• Initiating, responding and linking contributions to those of other speakers.
	• Maintaining and developing interaction, and negotiating.

Assessment notes

Model answers

The B2 First is usually taken by candidates who want to obtain a B2-level certificate, which corresponds to an upper-intermediate level of English. As described by the Common European Framework of Reference for Languages (CEFRL), candidates with a B2 level are considered *independent vantage users*, thus being able to understand the main ideas of complex tests, to interact with a certain degree of fluency and spontaneity both in written and oral form, and to produce clear and detailed texts on a range of subjects.

The purpose of the following model answers is to provide teachers and candidates with an example of language production and test performance that would score a high mark in a real B2 First Speaking test.

Without being particularly complex, these answers contain grammatical and lexical features as well as a range of discourse resources suited to an upper-intermediate level of English (B2). Please note that complete linguistic accuracy is not expected at B2 level, but only candidates whose performance is generally accurate will receive a high mark.

On page 94, to complement the answers, there are comments highlighting different aspects such as the strategies candidates make use of to address some of the parts, the way they express their opinions, how they interact with one another, etc. The aim of these comments is to draw the reader's attention to important details that might help to achieve a successful performance in this part of the B2 First examination.

Luis Porras Wadley

Granada, 2019

Luis Porras Wadley is the owner and director of KSE Academy, an English academy and official Cambridge English Exam Preparation Centre based in Granada. As an English teacher, Luis has been preparing Cambridge candidates successfully for over 8 years.
He is an author, EFL blogger, freelance writer and translator.

Test 1 – Part 1	Model answers
2 minutes (3 minutes for groups of three)	

Holidays and travelling

- **When was the last time that you went on holiday?** *The last time I was on holiday was last summer.* **(What did you do?)** *I went to Scotland for three days with my parents and we had a really good time.*
- **When you're on holiday, how do you like to travel?** *When I'm on holiday, I love travelling by plane and by train.* **(Why?)** *The plane is really fast, so it's great, and the best thing about the train is that you can enjoy the landscape while you travel.*
- **How often do you travel abroad?** *Maybe once a year, because I spend most of my summer holidays abroad.* **(Would you like to travel more?)** …… **(Why?)** *Of course. I think travelling's the best way to spend your holidays and you can learn a lot from it.*
- **Is there a country that you would really like to visit in the future?** *Yes, definitely, I'd love to visit Australia some day.* **(Why?)** *I believe it's a beautiful country with lots of things to see.*

Free time

- **How do you like to spend your free time?** …… **(Why?)** *I spend most of my free time with friends or watching TV at home.*
- **How much free time do you have?** *Not very much at the moment: I'm studying and I have a part-time job at the weekends, so I'm usually quite busy.* **(Do you think it's enough?)** *Not really. I mean, I'm fine with it, but sometimes I feel a little stressed and I would like to take some time off.*
- **Do you prefer to spend your free time alone or with friends?** …… **(Why?)** *I'd rather spend my time with friends, honestly. I think it's a lot more fun and interesting to do things with friends than alone.*
- **Is there a new leisure-time activity you'd like to try?** …… **(Which one?)** *Oh, yes. I'd love to try skiing. I've never done it before and I think I would enjoy it.* **(Why?)** *Well, I like snow and I already do snowboarding, so I believe skiing could be fun too.*

Television

- **Do you enjoy watching TV?** …… **(Why? / Why not?)** *No, not very much. Nowadays, I only watch series and films on my computer, because most of what there is on TV is quite boring.*
- **Do you think people spend too much time watching TV nowadays?** …… **(Why? / Why not?)** *Yes, for sure. Most people watch too much TV, and I think there are better things to do than watch TV all day long.*
- **Have you ever appeared on TV? (Tell us about it.)** *When I was a kid, I appeared once on TV. It was fun. I think a local TV station came to my school and they recorded us for one of their programmes, but I don't remember exactly why.*
- **Is there a programme you particularly enjoy watching?** …… **(Tell us about it.)** *Well, as I said before, I don't watch much TV, but if I have to say something, I do enjoy watching some animal documentaries from time to time. I love animals, and some of these documentaries are really well made.*

Model answers	Test 1 – Part 2
	4 minutes (6 minutes for groups of three)

1 Spending time together

Task 1 – Candidate A: What are the people enjoying about spending time together?

Both of these pictures show some people spending time together doing different things. In the first picture, we can see a family on the beach – it's actually a couple with a baby – whereas the second picture shows another couple, but, in this case, they seem to be moving into a new house – I think they're actually planning the decoration.

Obviously, the main difference between both pictures is where they're spending their time, given that in the first picture they're on the beach, while in the second they're at home. Moreover, the reason why they're spending time together is also completely different. On the one hand, the parents and the baby are spending some quality time together, as a family. The couple, on the other hand, are planning their new-house decoration, which is not a leisure-time activity. As for what they're enjoying, well, I suppose in both cases they just like spending time with each other and doing things together, but I would say that, in the second picture, they're also excited about their new home and starting a new life together.

Task 1 – Candidate B: Do you often spend time with your family?

Well, really, not as often as in the past. Nowadays, I'm studying in a different city and I'm not living with my parents at the moment, so I only spend time with them, maybe, a couple of times a month, when I go home for the weekend.

2 Eating out

Task 2 – Candidate B: Why have the people chosen to eat in these places?

Let me see… Okay, in the first picture, I can see a couple of women eating together in an office – I mean, I believe it's an office. They seem to be on their lunch break and they're probably colleagues. I think they're eating some Chinese or Japanese takeaway – they're using chopsticks – and they might not have enough time to go home to have lunch. Maybe their lunch break is not very long so they'd rather eat in the office.

The second picture is obviously very different because these people are in a pizza restaurant, not at work. They seem to be having a very good time, and they look younger than the women in the first picture – I think they're teenagers. I guess the reason for eating in that place is probably because they're celebrating someone's birthday, or maybe they are just enjoying lunch together as friends. I suppose they prefer going to a restaurant where their meal is served for them, instead of preparing something themselves at home.

Task 2 – Candidate A: Where do you usually eat with your friends?

Well, it depends, really. If it's just a regular weekend, we might go to a bar or an informal restaurant to grab a bite. However, if it's a special occasion, like someone's birthday, we'd probably have a barbecue in someone's house. I prefer barbecues, to be honest.

Test 1 – Part 3	Model answers
4 minutes (5 minutes for groups of three)	

Choosing a place to study

Task 3 – Candidates A & B: Talk to each other about the advantages and disadvantages of studying in these places.

Candidate A Would you like to start?

Candidate B Sure. Well, studying in your bedroom is usually a good idea because you're alone and there aren't many distractions. However, if you're alone with your laptop and your phone, it's extremely easy to get distracted, don't you think?

Candidate A Yes, you're absolutely right. You need to avoid that kind of distraction when you're studying on your own in your bedroom. As for studying in a friend's house, I believe it's okay for some tests, but maybe not for others. I mean, if it's something you need to learn by heart, studying with a friend is probably not the best choice. What do you think?

Candidate B I completely agree with you, but if it's something like maths or chemistry, you can help each other, right?

Candidate A Yes, exactly. And what about going to the library to study?

Candidate B Well, this is something that many people do, isn't it? I suppose it's because you need to be in silence and the atmosphere is suitable for studying. Don't you agree?

Candidate A Yes, it's probably one of the best options. The way I see it, it's much better than studying in the living room, isn't it?

Candidate B I was just going to say that. In my view, studying in the living room is a really bad idea, because, if there are other people at home, you will be distracted by the noise and you will be interrupted. And … how about the park?

Candidate A Well, I would never study in a park. I think the park's only good to spend your free time with friends, or maybe for reading.

Interlocutor: Thank you. Now you have about a minute to decide **what is the best place to study during exam periods**.

Candidate A Shall I start now?

Candidate B Yes, of course.

Candidate A Okay, if I had to choose one I would say that studying in your bedroom is probably the best option, or maybe in the library. What do you think?

Candidate B I'd rather study in the library. That way you can avoid some distractions like the laptop or your phone, don't you think?

Candidate A Yes, you may be right. That's probably the best option.

Candidate B Okay, so do we have an agreement?

Candidate A Yes, let's choose the library.

Model answers	Test 1 – Part 4
	4 minutes (6 minutes for groups of three)

- **Do you think that we study the right subjects at school?**
  …… (Why? / Why not?)

  Well, honestly, I think we study the right subjects, but probably not in the right way. What I mean is that while we need to study maths, history and other subjects like that, in my opinion, we should study them in a more practical way, not only memorising facts and stuff like that. I believe that's useless because after the test you just forget most of it.

- **Some people believe that practical experience is more useful than studying theory.**
  Do you agree? …… (Why? / Why not?)

  Yes, I completely agree. In my case, for instance, I can say I have learnt more by doing some training sessions with practical exercises than at home studying my notes. I think it's because practical experience is easier to remember in the long term – it's more memorable.

- **Do you believe teachers should be paid a higher salary than sportspeople?**
  …… (Why? / Why not?)

  Of course. I know that's impossible, but teachers do a more important job than people who do sport professionally. The problem is that nobody is interested in teachers, while millions of people support sports teams and players. I don't think it's fair.

- **Some people say that teachers and children get too many holidays.**
  What do you think?

  I don't agree at all. The truth is they spend many hours every day at school and that's not easy. I think teachers deserve their holidays, even more than the pupils. I suppose other workers are just green with envy, that's all.

- **Do you think that parents and teachers have the same responsibility in children's education?**
  …… (Why? / Why not?)

  No, I don't. This is a very difficult question, but I believe that both parents and teachers are responsible for children's education, but in different ways. Parents ought to teach children to be good people, responsible and hardworking, whereas teachers should only be responsible for teaching them the different subjects. However, the situation is much more complex than that.

- **Some people say that it's more important to study science than history.**
  What's your opinion?

  Actually, I agree with that. I believe that we have to study history, as we must understand our past, but, on the other hand, I suppose that scientific progress is more important than that. So yeah, I'd say that science is more important than history.

Model answers – Part 1 – examiner's comments

In Part 1, candidates are asked about themselves, their background and experiences. Candidates are expected to expand on their answers, but these should not turn into a monologue. If the answer given to a question is particularly short, if appropriate, the examiner will probably ask a follow-up question. For example:

Main question	***How often do you travel abroad?***
	Maybe once a year, because I spend most of my summer holidays abroad.
Follow-up question	***Would you like to travel more?***
	Of course. I think travelling's the best way to spend your holidays and you can learn a lot from it.

These questions are scripted and the interlocutor will never improvise them. Given the nature of the conversation, these answers should sound natural and non-rehearsed. For example:

Main question	***Is there a new leisure-time activity you'd like to try? .... (Which one?)***
	Oh, yes! I'd love to try skiing. I've never done it before and I think I would enjoy it.
Follow-up question	***Why?***
	Well, I like the snow and I already do snowboarding, so I believe skiing could be fun too.

Sounding natural is part of being fluent in a language, so using some informal expressions (*Oh*), exclamations, contractions (*I'd love to*) or discourse markers *(Well)* is actually encouraged.

As for rehearsed answers, examiners expect that some of the candidates' answers might sound rehearsed, but if they are lengthy and sound too unnatural, candidates might be politely interrupted.

As this is a B2-level speaking test, candidates' answers should show B2-level grammar and vocabulary, even in Part 1. For this reason, in the model answers provided for Part 1, there are some appropriate-level phrases like:

> *I'd rather spend my time with friends ... Nowadays, ... take some time off ... a part-time job ... the best thing about the train is that ... Yes, definitely, ...*

Part 1 is probably not the most suitable part for candidates to prove their level, but they should still try to show what they know.

Model answers – Part 2 – examiner's comments

In Part 2, each candidate is asked to compare two pictures and answer a question about them. Also, they will have to answer a follow-up question regarding their partner's pictures. This is a chance for candidates to show how well they can speak on their own in a longer turn. For this reason, not only are candidates' grammar and vocabulary expected to be good, but there is special emphasis on their discourse management – i.e. how long they can speak for, how relevant their contributions are and how well they organise their speech.

The language candidates use

If we take a look at Candidate A's and Candidate B's comparisons, we notice that they:

- **use appropriate B2 grammar and vocabulary:**

    it's actually a couple with a baby ... they seem to be moving into a new house ... given that... a leisure-time activity ... quality time ... starting a new life together ... takeaway ... chopsticks ... they might not have enough time to go home ... they'd rather eat in the office ... they look younger than ... I guess the reason for ... their meal is served for them ... instead of preparing something themselves ... etc.

- **use cohesive devices and discourse markers to organise his/her speech:**

    Both of these pictures ... In the first picture ... whereas the second picture shows ... ... while ... Moreover, ... On the one hand, ... On the other hand, ... As for ... Let me see, ... I mean, ... etc.

- **not only describe, but rather speculate:**

    I believe ... They seem to be ... I think ... They might not have ... Maybe ... I suppose ... I would say ... etc.

How candidates organise their speech

It's also important to notice how both candidates organise their speech as they use different strategies to approach this part of the test.

On the one hand, Candidate A chooses to briefly describe both pictures first. Then he/she compares them, pointing out the main differences and, finally, he/she addresses the question directly (*What are the people enjoying about spending time together?*).

On the other hand, Candidate B uses a different strategy, focusing on each picture separately, describing each picture more thoroughly, comparing the second picture with the first, and providing an answer to the question (*Why have the people chosen to eat in these places?*) for each picture.

Both ways of doing this task are perfectly fine, but candidates need to know that some comparison and speculation is essential – rather than providing a simple description of both pictures – and that they have up to 60 seconds to provide their answers.

Follow-up question

The follow-up question is always related to the topic of the pictures. In fact, sometimes candidates will be asked to choose the most suitable one with regard to their preferences.

The answer should normally be addressed from a personal point of view and it should expand beyond a one-phrase sentence.

Candidates have up to 30 seconds to provide a suitable answer to the follow-up question and, if appropriate, it is advisable that they make the most of that time.

Model answers – Part 3 – examiner's comments

In Part 3, candidates will hold a conversation about a topic that is presented in the form of a question and some prompts that provide ideas for this conversation. For this reason, Part 3 is the main collaborative task of the exam, as it is to be carried out in pairs.

The main purpose of this part of the test is to see how well candidates can interact with each other by discussing and exchanging views and opinions, asking for opinions, justifying their answers, agreeing and disagreeing with each other, reaching agreements, making decisions, etc.

Notice the following elements in the sample answer on page X:

- **Expressing views and opinions:**

    is usually a good idea … you need to avoid … I believe it's okay to … that's probably one of the best options … the way I see it … In my view … I'd rather study … I would never study … I think the park is …

- **Asking for opinions:**

    don't you think? … What do you think? … right? … And what about…? … Don't you agree? … isn't it? … how about…? … do we have an agreement?

- **Agreeing and disagreeing:**

    Yes, you're absolutely right … I completely agree with you … Yes, exactly … I was just going to say that … Yeah, you may be right … I'd rather …

All of these expressions show that candidates are capable of initiating, responding and linking contributions to each other's turn, and that they can develop a successful interaction and negotiate towards an outcome.

Finally, it is extremely important that this part does not turn into two separate, individual turns at speaking rather than a seamless interaction.

Therefore, candidates should avoid lengthy answers and should try to involve their partner at the end of each turn.

Model answers – Part 4 – examiner's comments

In Part 4, candidates are asked questions that stem from the topic developed in Part 3. These are usually more complex questions and they will have to answer them either individually or as a short conversation with their partner.

The main goal of this part is to produce longer stretches of language in which candidates show their ability to discuss a topic to a more complex extent. It is, therefore, a great opportunity for candidates to give answers that are organised and insightful, and to make sure that their grammar and vocabulary are as good as that expected for a B2-level exam.

Some examples of good answers are as follows:

> ***Do you think that we study the right subjects at school? …… (Why? / Why not?)***

> *Well, honestly, I think we study the right subjects, but probably not in the right way. What I mean is that while we need to study maths, history and other subjects like that, in my opinion, we should study them in a more practical way, not only memorising facts and stuff like that. I believe that's useless because after the test you just forget most of it.*

The candidate is expanding on his/her initial premise (*I think we study the right subjects, but probably not in the right way*) by using a phrasal discourse marker like "*What I mean is that…*". Also, the language used is usually appropriate (*in a more practical way … not only memorising facts … that's useless … forget most of it*), but also natural (*honestly … stuff like that*).

> ***Some people say that teachers and children get too many holidays. What do you think?***

> *I don't agree at all. The truth is they spend many hours every day at school and that's not easy. I think teachers deserve their holidays, even more than the pupils. I suppose other workers are just green with envy, that's all.*

In this case, the candidate is clearly and strongly disagreeing with the statement provided by the examiner (*I don't agree at all*), and then justifying it (*The truth is … I think … I suppose*). Also, apart from suitable grammar and vocabulary, he/she uses an idiomatic expression (*green with envy*). Although idioms are not essential to obtain a good mark, they are expected at a strong B2 level.

Some people say that it's more important to study science than history. What's your opinion?
Actually, I agree with that. I believe that we have to study history, as we must understand our past, but, on the other hand, I suppose that scientific progress is more important than that. So yeah, I'd say that science is more important than history.

This is also a good answer for several reasons: it features good grammar, like the correct use of modal verbs (*must understand*), great organisation (*But on the other hand,*), speculation (*I suppose ... I'd say*) and a natural-sounding 'round-off' answer (*So yeah, I'd say that ...*).

www.ingramcontent.com/pod-product-compliance
Lightning Source LLC
Chambersburg PA
CBHW081353080526
44588CB00016B/2483